GENIUS!

THE MOST ASTONISHING INVENTIONS OF ALL TIME

DEBORAH KESPERT

GENIUS!

THE MOST ASTONISHING INVENTIONS OF ALL TIME

Thames & Hudson

CONTENTS

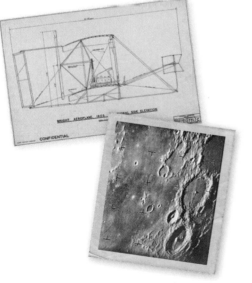

GREAT INVENTIONS

 Since ancient times, human beings have been inspired to invent tools and machines to improve their lives. Here are just some of the incredible inventions in history that have helped to shape the world today.

c. 3500 BCE

Wheel
In Mesopotamia, near modern-day Iraq, the ancient Sumerians build wheeled carts.

c. 3000 BCE

Lever
This simple bar on a hinge is possibly first used in ancient Egypt. It helps people to lift and move heavy objects, such as stones, more easily.

c. 2300 BCE

Abacus
The ancient Sumerians devise a tool for counting. Early abacuses use rows of marks or beads to work out sums.

c. 240 BCE

Archimedes screw
Ancient Greek genius Archimedes builds a screw that pumps water uphill. The device is still used today.

200 BCE – 200 CE

Compass
The Chinese discover a magnetic stone that swings to point south. They use it for fortune-telling. In the 1200s they make compasses for navigating.

c. 1439

Printing press
Johannes Gutenberg builds a printing press with movable, reusable type. It makes books easily and cheaply available to the world.

1608

Telescope
Hans Lippershey describes a telescope, which astronomer Galileo Galilei later improves and uses to study space.

telescope

c. 1752

Lightning conductor
Benjamin Franklin invents the lightning conductor, which guides electrical currents to the ground during storms.

c. 1765

Steam engine
James Watt builds an efficient steam engine to power machines. It starts the growth of factories around the world.

1885

Motor car
Karl Benz builds the first useful motor car. Three years later his wife, Bertha, takes it for a long drive and shows its benefits to the world.

motor car

1895

Cinema
The Lumière Brothers make a machine that can film and project moving pictures to an audience. They create the cinema.

cinema

1901

Radio telegraph
Guglielmo Marconi transmits a long-distance wireless message by radio telegraph.

1939

Bombe machine
Alan Turing designs a complex code-breaking machine during wartime. He goes on to develop the first computers.

1964

Personal computer
Pier Giorgio Perotto launches a personal computer that fits on a desk.

personal computer

1965

Kevlar
Stephanie Kwolek invents kevlar, a material five times stronger than steel. It is made into life-saving clothes that protect against fire and bullets.

1969

***Saturn V* rocket**
Astronauts blast off to the Moon in a spacecraft launched by Wernher von Braun's engineering marvel, the *Saturn V* rocket.

The color tells you the kind of invention you are looking at. A pioneer is a person working in a new area of knowledge.

CE stands for Common Era. The Common Era begins in the first century with year 1. The time before that is known as BCE, which stands for Before The Common Era.

c. stands for circa, which means approximately.

⚙ PIONEERS

((ɸ)) COMMUNICATION

⏻ TECHNOLOGY

◎ TRANSPORT

📡 INTO SPACE

105
Paper
In China, Cai Lun improves paper by pulping rags and plant fibers, pressing them into sheets and then hanging them out to dry.

132
Earthquake detector
Zhang Heng builds the first earthquake detector. It makes a noise by dropping a metal ball when an earthquake occurs.

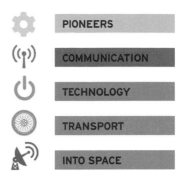
earthquake detector

c.800 - 900
Gunpowder
The Chinese develop gunpowder, an explosive mixture. They use it to make fireworks, rockets and weapons.

c.1200
Elephant clock
Al-Jazari designs a water clock to mark time. Water clocks have been around since ancient times, but al-Jazari's is an engineering marvel.

1783
Hot-air balloon
The Montgolfier Brothers' hot-air balloon takes to the air with passengers. It is the first time humans fly successfully.

1829
Steam train
George and Robert Stephenson build the *Rocket*, the fastest steam locomotive of its day. The railways grow in size and importance.

1876
Telephone
Alexander Graham Bell and Elisha Gray rush to register their telephone designs. The telephone becomes a new way to communicate.

telephone

1879
Light bulb
Thomas Edison makes a practical long-lasting light bulb and provides electric power on a large scale.

1903
Airplane
The Wright Brothers make the first controlled flight in a powered airplane, over 400 years after Leonardo da Vinci sketches his flying machines.

airplane

1926
Television
John Logie Baird builds a working TV set and shows it to the public. He helps to make TV popular.

1933
Radio telescope
Karl Jansky builds an instrument to collect radio waves and tells the world about signals coming from space.

radio telescope

1973
Mobile phone
In the United States, Martin Cooper makes the first call from a handheld cell phone. By the mid-1990s mobile phones are popular devices.

1991
World Wide Web
Tim Berners-Lee invents the World Wide Web for everyone to use. It changes the way we share information.

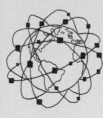
World Wide Web

2012
PillCam
Scientists devise a new way to examine parts of your body from the inside. It's a tiny camera in the form of a pill.

2014
DNA test kit
Chris Toumazou invents a kit that can test if you might get a particular illness. It is like a tiny lab on a memory stick. It may prevent diseases in the future.

MARVELOUS MACHINES

THE BIG IDEA	⟫ To build simple and ingenious devices, including an invention that could carry water up a hill.

CHALLENGES Only simple tools and materials; lived in dangerous war-torn times	**WHAT ARCHIMEDES SCREW** **WHO** Archimedes **WHERE** Syracuse, an ancient Greek city in modern-day Sicily, Italy **WHEN** 3rd century BCE **HOW** it is likely he studied other devices and improved them **WHY** to pump dirty water out of the hold, or bottom, of a huge ship
BACKGROUND	Archimedes probably spent time studying in Egypt. He then went home to Syracuse to work for King Hiero II. Here, he worked obsessively on his ideas and came up with brilliant inventions.

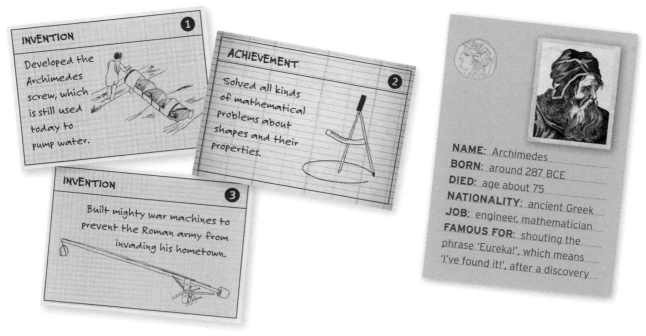

INVENTION ①

Developed the Archimedes screw, which is still used today to pump water.

ACHIEVEMENT ②

Solved all kinds of mathematical problems about shapes and their properties.

INVENTION ③

Built mighty war machines to prevent the Roman army from invading his hometown.

NAME: Archimedes
BORN: around 287 BCE
DIED: age about 75
NATIONALITY: ancient Greek
JOB: engineer, mathematician
FAMOUS FOR: shouting the phrase 'Eureka!', which means 'I've found it!', after a discovery

→ Archimedes probably made models to explore how things worked and to test out his theories. These models used levers and pulleys, which he studied in great depth.

MARVELOUS MACHINES

›› King Hiero of Syracuse had a problem. Could Archimedes solve it?

›› HOW TO ...

Make a Water Screw
You will need: plastic pipe · flexible, see-through tubing · two bowls · poster paint · books · tape

❶ Fill one bowl with water and color it with poster paint.

❷ Place on a table. Stand the other bowl on a pile of books.

❸ Wind the tubing around the pipe and tape them together.

❹ Stand the device in the bowl of water. Lean the higher end against the other bowl.

❺ Turn the pipe and watch the water rise!

↑ This modern-day Archimedes screw is part of a pumping station in the Netherlands. The pumping station drains water from land that was once under the sea to create areas called polders. The Dutch have reclaimed lots of land for farming in this way.

Archimedes was one of the most famous mathematicians and inventors of ancient times. Using his razor-sharp brain, he developed pulleys that would haul large objects and he explained how levers could lift heavy weights. People said that he was so obsessed with his work that he drew diagrams on his body and forgot to eat! He lived a long time ago and we can't be sure that all the incredible stories are true, but we do know that his brilliant problem-solving, methodical approach and extensive writings helped to change the way people thought about science.

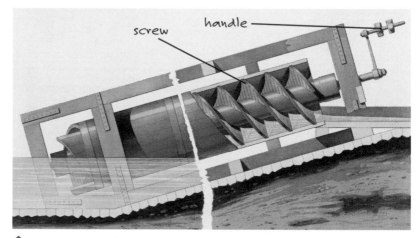

↑ Here you can see what the inside of an Archimedes screw looks like.

One story tells us how Archimedes invented his most famous device – the Archimedes screw. King Hiero II of Syracuse needed a giant wooden ship to carry 600 soldiers. Nobody had made a ship that big before. How would it get into the sea? Archimedes had the answer. He built the ship, named *Syracusia*, and launched it into the water with a complicated system of levers and pulleys.

But water seeps into wooden ships between the joints. Unless the crew could pump it out, the ship was sure to sink. Archimedes solved this problem with his water screw, which was a screw inside a tube with a handle. When you turned the handle, the screw scooped up water from the bottom of the ship and carried it to the top so that it could pour out.

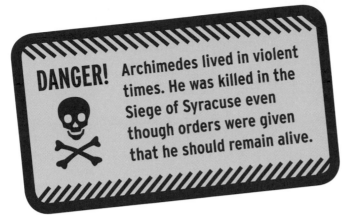

DANGER! Archimedes lived in violent times. He was killed in the Siege of Syracuse even though orders were given that he should remain alive.

In ancient times, farmers used screw-like devices to lift water from rivers for their crops. Archimedes may have seen them, then improved them to make his own water screw. More than 2,000 years after Archimedes's time, the machine he gave his name to is still a vital piece of equipment. Modern-day versions of the Archimedes screw help to prevent flooding, pump away sewage and even transport fish safely from one place to another.

Archimedes is also well known for working out a way to measure the volume of an object, which is how much space it takes up. A famous story tells us that he was in a public bath when he made this discovery. He suddenly realized that he could drop an object into a vessel full of water and measure how much water spilled out. The amount of spilled-out water was the same as the volume of the object. It is said that Archimedes, thrilled by the discovery, jumped out of the bath and ran down the street completely naked!

⬆ Legend has it that Archimedes shouted 'Eureka', which means 'I've found it', when he jumped out of his bath. This probably isn't actually true, but people still use this phrase today when they solve a tricky problem.

EXTRA

WEAPONS FOR BATTLE

Ancient writers claimed that Archimedes created mighty war machines to help smash the Romans.

The **Archimedes claw** was a huge crane with a hook at the end. The hook grabbed ships and pulled them out of the water, making them tilt and sink.

Archimedes did not invent the **catapult**, but there are reports that he improved the design so that it could fire large stones over longer distances more accurately.

According to ancient legends, the **Archimedes death ray** was a set of large mirrors or polished shields that reflected the Sun's light onto enemy ships and made them burst into flames.

DETECTING EARTHQUAKES

THE BIG IDEA	⟫ To invent a clever mechanical device that could tell if there was an earthquake and which direction it was coming from.
CHALLENGES No one knew what caused earthquakes; enemies claimed that the device did not work	**WHAT EARTHQUAKE DETECTOR** **WHO** Zhang Heng **WHERE** China **WHEN** Around 132 CE **HOW** he was skilled at working with moving parts and gears **WHY** he was fascinated by the Earth, planets, Moon and stars
BACKGROUND	Zhang Heng lived during the Han Dynasty (206 BCE to 220 CE). At this time, China was far ahead of Europe in developing machines. He worked for two Emperors as Chief Astronomer and was also a poet.

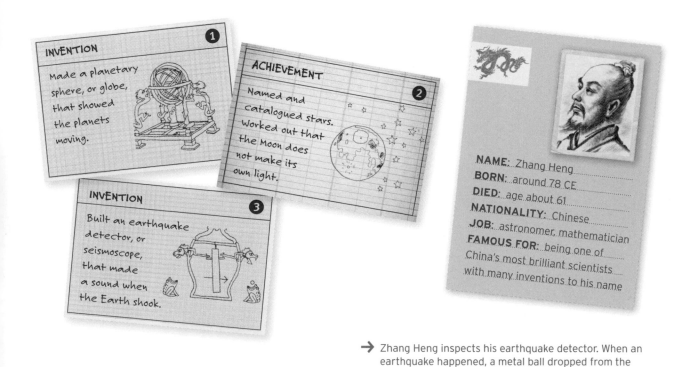

INVENTION ❶

Made a planetary sphere, or globe, that showed the planets moving.

ACHIEVEMENT ❷

Named and catalogued stars. Worked out that the Moon does not make its own light.

INVENTION ❸

Built an earthquake detector, or seismoscope, that made a sound when the Earth shook.

NAME: Zhang Heng
BORN: around 78 CE
DIED: age about 61
NATIONALITY: Chinese
JOB: astronomer, mathematician
FAMOUS FOR: being one of China's most brilliant scientists with many inventions to his name

→ Zhang Heng inspects his earthquake detector. When an earthquake happened, a metal ball dropped from the mouth of a dragon into a frog and made a loud clang.

張衡候風地動儀

DETECTING
EARTHQUAKES

↑ Heng's trundle cart had a wooden figure who banged a drum every time the cart traveled one 'li' (about 500 m or 1,640 ft). By counting the number of times the drum banged, you could work out the distance covered.

▶▶ HOW ...

An Earthquake is Measured
There are several scales to measure the power of earthquakes. The Mercalli Scale records the amount of damage you can see and feel.

I	Not felt
II	Felt but no damage
III–IV	Objects shake indoors
V–VI	Objects break, slight damage to buildings
VII–VIII	Hard to stand, heavier damage to buildings
IX–X	Bridges collapse
XI–XII	Few or no buildings left

▶▶ What new mechanical marvel would Zhang Heng show to the Emperor?

When Zhang Heng presented his beautiful metal earthquake detector to the Emperor, he already had a long track record as an incredible inventor. He had designed a globe to show the movement of the planets and the stars, improved the design of the water clock and built a mechanical trundle cart that could measure the distance a vehicle traveled. He had also developed all kinds of complicated mathematical calculations, planned calendars and written poetry. In short, Zhang Heng was an all-round genius.

His latest revolutionary device was shaped like a vase with dragon heads at the top and frogs at the bottom. Inside, a pendulum, or swinging weight, moved when the Earth shook and sent a ball from one of the dragons into a frog's mouth. Depending on which frog the ball fell into, you could tell which direction the earthquake was coming from.

In ancient China, people feared earthquakes hugely and believed that they were punishments from the heavens. Today, we know that an earthquake is a shaking of the Earth's crust caused by movements in the giant plates on which our continents and oceans sit.

↑ Many modern buildings, like these tall office blocks and skyscrapers in Taiwan, are designed to stay up when an earthquake occurs.

↑ This scientist is using modern-day earthquake detection equipment. The lines on the printout show that there are strong vibrations beneath the ground.

The first time Zhang Heng demonstrated his machine, it sprang into action. But no one felt the ground tremble, so his enemies said that it didn't work. Then several days later, a messenger arrived announcing that there had indeed been an earthquake about 500 km (310 miles) away in the direction indicated by the machine.

Zhang Heng's machine could not predict when an earthquake was going to happen, and even today predicting earthquakes is difficult. But we do have modern equipment called seismometers that record vibrations in the Earth. When the vibrations increase, it means an earthquake is more likely.

Although Zhang Heng's device was simple by modern standards, it was incredible for its time. What's more, no one else managed to make an effective earthquake detector until the 18th century – more than 1,500 years later.

DANGER! Many earthquakes have hit China, including the world's deadliest earthquake. It took place in 1556 and killed over 800,000 people.

EXTRA

CHINESE FIRSTS

The ancient Chinese invented many things that we still use in one form or another today.

Between 200 BCE and 200 CE, the first **compass** was built. It was a large spoon made from magnetic lodestone with a handle that spun to point south.

Between 800 and 900, the Chinese discovered **gunpowder**. This highly explosive mix led to the invention of fireworks and powerful weapons such as rockets.

Today, people fly **kites** for fun but in China the first kites probably had a practical use. Early Chinese writings describe them carrying messages, measuring distances and testing wind strength.

MECHANICAL WONDERS

THE BIG IDEA	›› To build a giant water-powered clock that could keep time and entertain people.

CHALLENGES

Keeping time accurately; getting lots of intricate parts to work together smoothly

WHAT ELEPHANT CLOCK
WHO al-Jazari
WHERE Diyarbakir, a city in what is now southeastern Turkey
WHEN around 1200
HOW he combined a practical mind with a brilliant imagination
WHY to let people know when it was time to say prayers

BACKGROUND

Al-Jazari was a Muslim inventor who lived during a 'golden age' of Islamic scientific discoveries. He worked for 30 years at Artuklu Palace as chief engineer to several Muslim rulers.

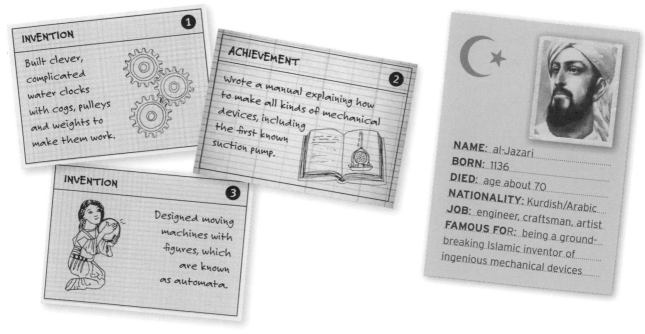

INVENTION ❶
Built clever, complicated water clocks with cogs, pulleys and weights to make them work.

ACHIEVEMENT ❷
Wrote a manual explaining how to make all kinds of mechanical devices, including the first known suction pump.

INVENTION ❸
Designed moving machines with figures, which are known as automata.

NAME: al-Jazari
BORN: 1136
DIED: age about 70
NATIONALITY: Kurdish/Arabic
JOB: engineer, craftsman, artist
FAMOUS FOR: being a groundbreaking Islamic inventor of ingenious mechanical devices

→ Hidden inside al-Jazari's mechanical elephant is a water clock. He describes how it works in *The Book of Knowledge of Ingenious Mechanical Devices*.

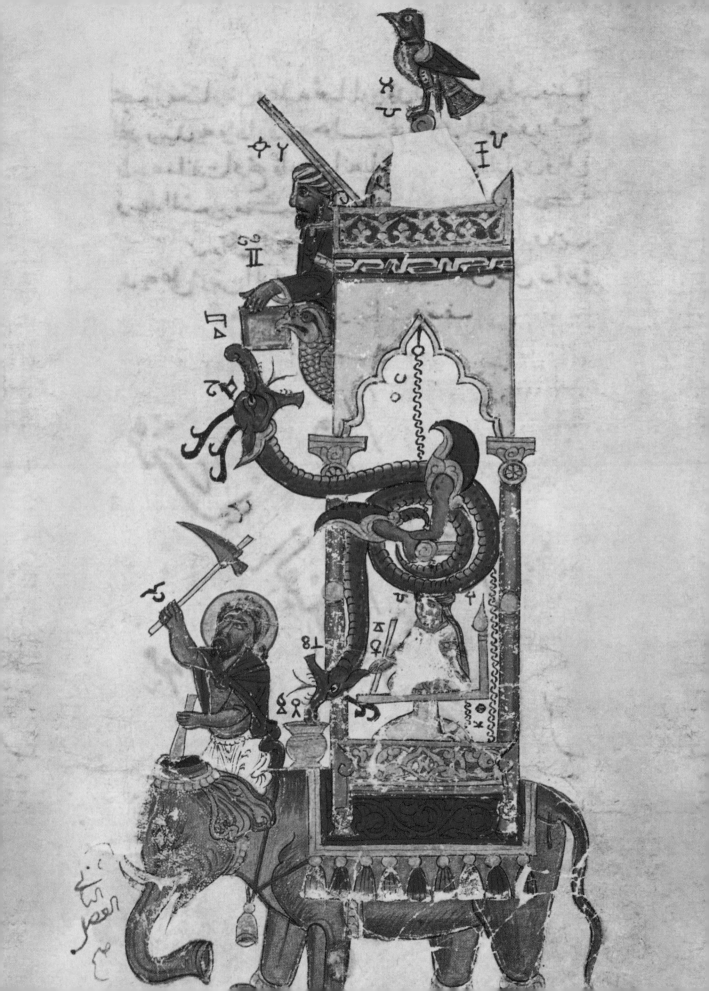

>> **Al-Jazari picked up his pen and began to write down his life's work ...**

At the beginning of the 13th century, the Muslim ruler Nasir al-Din Mahmud asked his chief engineer, al-Jazari, to write a book. He wanted it to describe all the extraordinary machines al-Jazari had created during the years he worked for the court. It was known as *The Book of Knowledge of Ingenious Mechanical Devices*. The book gave instructions on how to build 50 mechanical marvels and was packed with technical diagrams. One of the most complicated, beautiful and useful machines was al-Jazari's large elephant clock.

The movements of the clock were controlled by a bowl floating in a tank of water. In the base of the bowl, there was a small hole so that it would fill with water and sink. As the bowl slowly sank over half an hour, it tugged a system of pulleys that moved a writer and his pen to mark the minutes. After half an hour, the bowl completely sank to the bottom of the tank, and pulled a rope attached to a seesaw mechanism in the clock tower. This triggered a ball to fall from the mouth of a serpent into a vase. It reset the bowl and at the same time made a rider bang the elephant's head and a bird spin around. The hours were marked by a dial at the top of the clock.

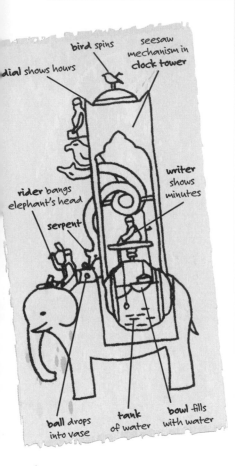

bird spins

seesaw mechanism in clock tower

dial shows hours

writer shows minutes

rider bangs elephant's head

serpent

ball drops into vase

tank of water

bowl fills with water

↑ Here you can see inside the elephant clock and how its parts worked.

↑ Al-Jazari's castle clock was even more complex than his elephant clock. Automatic gates opened to mark each hour while musicians played below. A dial on top showed the position of the stars and Moon.

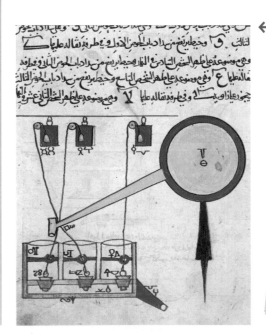

← The diagrams in al-Jazari's book were so detailed that people can build models of his machines today. This diagram shows a mechanism inside one of his clocks.

The Book of Knowledge of Ingenious Mechanical Devices contained among other things ...

- candle and water clocks
- a mechanical peacock
- automatic gates
- a combination lock
- shape-changing water fountains

In the Islamic world, timekeeping is important for religious reasons as well as in daily life. People say prayers at set times of the day. This made al-Jazari's clock a vital piece of equipment. Al-Jazari invented other important machines too, such as devices that raised water to irrigate crops. But some of his inventions, such as a boat with robotic musicians and a waitress that poured drinks, were purely for entertainment.

↑ This is a model of al-Jazari's suction pump. It was powered by a water wheel and worked by sucking up water through the pipes to an outlet at the top.

beam with movable pegs

↑ Al-Jazari's musical boat had pegs that hit levers to work the musicians. The position of the pegs could be changed to program the musicians to play different rhythms.

↑ The robot waitress poured drinks to amuse guests at parties. In this illustration, al-Jazari shows how her arm moves.

What made al-Jazari's machines special was the way they worked. He cleverly connected cogs, levers, shafts and cranks in ways that no one had done before. He was the first person to describe a crankshaft. This simple device turned circular movement into up-and-down movement and vice-versa. It was vital for the development of the steam engine over 500 years later and is still used in car engines today. Al-Jazari also invented the first known suction pump and simple programmable robots.

↑ Today, we can program robots to carry out all kinds of jobs. Robonaut 2 lives on the International Space Station, helping astronauts with repetitive or dangerous tasks.

Little is known about al-Jazari's life and none of his machines have survived. But the remarkable encyclopedia of inventions completed shortly before his death in 1206 is still here to remind us that he was a genius engineer.

DESIGNS AHEAD OF HIS TIME

THE BIG IDEA	» To design astonishing machines that would allow human beings to take to the air and fly.

CHALLENGES	**WHAT ORNITHOPTER AND HELICOPTER**
	WHO Leonardo da Vinci
	WHERE Vinci, present-day Italy
Getting a flying machine off the ground before the engine had been invented	**WHEN** 1480s
	HOW he studied how birds flew and sketched their wings
	WHY he was obsessed with the idea of flight from an early age

BACKGROUND	Da Vinci trained as a painter and soon became famous because he was so talented. Throughout his life, he furiously filled notebooks with designs for different inventions.

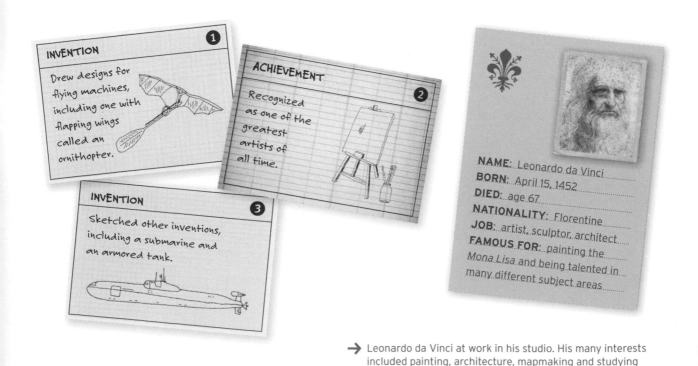

INVENTION ❶
Drew designs for flying machines, including one with flapping wings called an ornithopter.

ACHIEVEMENT ❷
Recognized as one of the greatest artists of all time.

INVENTION ❸
Sketched other inventions, including a submarine and an armored tank.

NAME: Leonardo da Vinci
BORN: April 15, 1452
DIED: age 67
NATIONALITY: Florentine
JOB: artist, sculptor, architect
FAMOUS FOR: painting the Mona Lisa and being talented in many different subject areas

→ Leonardo da Vinci at work in his studio. His many interests included painting, architecture, mapmaking and studying the Earth and the human body.

≫ Would da Vinci achieve his dream and build a machine that could fly?

During the 15th century, while Leonardo da Vinci painted fabulous works of art and was admired for his wide-ranging talents, he was also trying to fulfill a dream. He wanted to build a flying machine. Stories tell us that a bird landed on his cradle as a baby and its tail feathers brushed his face. Could this have inspired his obsession with flight?

↑ In 1503, da Vinci started work on the *Mona Lisa*. It is probably the world's most famous painting. Only about 15 of da Vinci's paintings survive today.

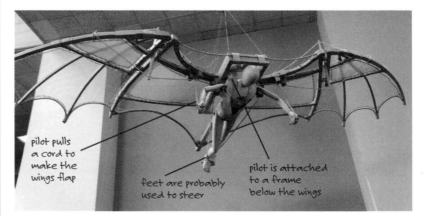

pilot pulls a cord to make the wings flap

feet are probably used to steer

pilot is attached to a frame below the wings

↑ A model of da Vinci's ornithopter, on display in the National Library of Spain. Da Vinci's wing designs were inspired by bats, birds and toy kites.

For decades, da Vinci studied the movement of birds, drew sketches and experimented with different designs. In secret, he recorded these ideas in notebooks, making more than 500 drawings on the topic. He came up with designs for lots of other things too, including a giant crossbow, a submarine, a robot knight that could lift its helmet and an ideal city for the future. By the time he died, he had filled over 13,000 pages.

Da Vinci's notebooks were not published during his lifetime, neither were they bound like the books we know today. Instead, they were loose sheets of paper bundled together in cloth. They were difficult to read because he used a special back-to-front mirror writing to keep important ideas secret.

MIRROR WRITING

In mirror writing, the letters are written backward and you read from left to right.

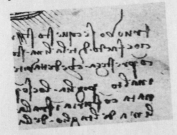

To read the example below, turn the book away from you, then hold up a mirror to the page. Try out mirror writing. It might be easier if you are left-handed like da Vinci.

ɿɔniV ɒb obɿɒnoɘ⅃
¡sᴉuᴉǝƃ ɐ sɐʍ

Leonardo da Vinci said
'For once you have tasted flight, you will walk the Earth with your eyes turned skywards, for there you have been and there you will long to return.'

When da Vinci died, pages fell into the hands of friends and collectors. In 1966, two notebooks turned up in a museum in Spain, more than 500 years after he had written them!

One of da Vinci's ideas for a flying machine was a bird-like contraption with mechanical flapping wings operated by a human being. Today, we call a machine like this an ornithopter. Da Vinci came up with several designs for ornithopters. Sometimes people flew standing up, other times they lay flat. In one version, a person hung beneath the wings pulling levers and cords with their hands and feet to make them flap. In another, the person wore a head harness to steer. He had a machine shaped like a boat and even one with a ladder that would fold up after takeoff.

↑ A modern-day helicopter usually has four narrow blades on top to provide lift. Tail blades stop the helicopter from spinning round in the air.

Around the same time, da Vinci sketched a different kind of flying machine. This one had a spinning wing on top and lifted straight off the ground. It was the first design for a helicopter. No one is really sure but da Vinci's idea may have been inspired by the seeds of the sycamore tree, which whirl as they fall, or perhaps an Archimedes screw (see pages 8 to 11). The first working helicopters were not mass-produced until the 1940s, almost 500 years after da Vinci's sketch.

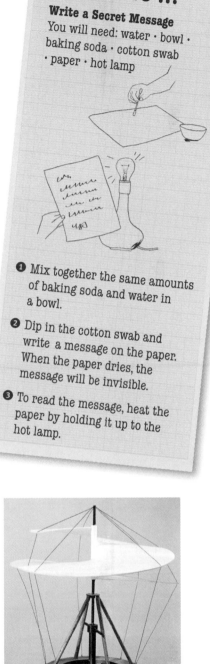

▶▶ **HOW TO ...**

Write a Secret Message

You will need: water · bowl · baking soda · cotton swab · paper · hot lamp

❶ Mix together the same amounts of baking soda and water in a bowl.

❷ Dip in the cotton swab and write a message on the paper. When the paper dries, the message will be invisible.

❸ To read the message, heat the paper by holding it up to the hot lamp.

↑ Da Vinci's helicopter is known as the airscrew. The idea was that two people stood on the base and turned a handle. This would make the screw-like wing on top spin around and give the helicopter the power to take off.

≫ Would da Vinci achieve his dream and build a machine that could fly?

Leonardo da Vinci's flying machines were wildly imaginative, but there was a big problem. They were too heavy. Even with ropes, cranks and pulleys, a human being could never produce enough power to get them off the ground. His ornithopter had giant flapping wings. That was fine for birds and bats with light bodies and powerful muscles designed for flying, but not for humans with heavy bodies designed for walking. Today, airplanes are powered by engines, but engines had not yet been invented. The technology to make da Vinci's machines fly did not exist.

No one is sure if da Vinci ever tried to build his flying machines. He may have made models using materials available at the time, such as wood for the wing frames and starched cloth or parchment for the wings. There are rumors that he even tested an ornithopter in secret. Around 1505 he wrote, 'The great bird will take its first flight upon the back of the great swan, filling the whole world with amazement and filling all records with its fame'. But the truth is flying his ornithopter would have ended in disaster.

↑ A parachute with a pyramid-shaped top appears in one of da Vinci's notebooks. In 2008, a Swiss skydiver tested this design. It worked perfectly even though the landing was bumpy.

↑ It is said that Leonardo da Vinci was a vegetarian and loved animals. He bought caged birds from the market so that he could set them free.

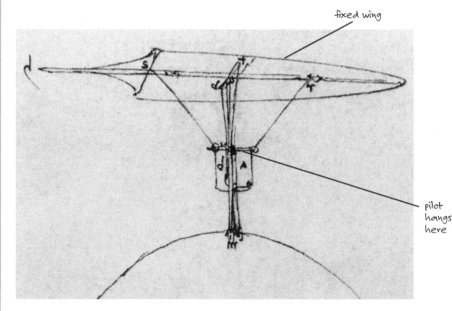

fixed wing

pilot hangs here

↑ Da Vinci's sketch for a glider. It is similar to a modern-day hang glider with the pilot holding on below the wing. In 2002, a paraglider successfully flew a machine based on this drawing, after adding a tail for stability.

↑ People continue to push the boundaries of science and adventure. A wingsuit lets a skydiver fly through the air before he or she lands with a parachute.

Da Vinci never gave up his obsession. He realized that he needed extra power and experimented with springs. He also developed new wing designs. Toward the end of his life, he devoted a whole notebook to flight, known as the *Codex on the Flight of Birds*. In it, he observed how birds glided and balanced. He thought about the forces produced by a wing in the air and how a pilot might control the plane. He even sketched a cockpit. Finally, he decided that he needed a lighter craft and that a fixed wing would be better than a flapping one. Four hundred years later, in 1903, Orville and Wilbur Wright (see pages 74 to 79) used similar ideas to build a fixed-wing airplane with an engine and make the first ever successful powered flight.

Imagine if Leonardo da Vinci was alive today and walked with his 'eyes turned skywards'. He might see skydivers making daredevil parachute jumps, helicopters reporting on traffic conditions or passenger planes flying to far-off places. He would discover that his sketches had flown in a space probe to Mars and were wandering around the surface of the planet in the Curiosity rover! How might he feel to know that after all this time his dreams about flying had become real?

EXTRA

FULL OF IDEAS

Da Vinci's notebooks showed sketches for inventions next to recipes and shopping lists.

This design for an **armored tank** had cannons attached to a round platform. It could travel in any direction. Armored tanks were first used and developed during World War I (1914–18).

Da Vinci's **diving equipment** consisted of a face mask with two air tubes attached to a bell-shaped float on the surface of the water. He also described air tanks. Self-contained air tanks appeared in the 1860s.

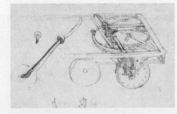

Da Vinci drew a sketch for a **three-wheeled car** powered by springs and with brakes 400 years before the motor car was invented. (See pages 70 to 73.)

THE FIRST PRINTING PRESS

THE BIG IDEA	» To print books in Europe for the first time in history, making learning and reading available to everyone.

CHALLENGES	**WHAT** THE FIRST PRINTING PRESS
	WHO Johannes Gutenberg
	WHERE Mainz, present-day Germany
Had to borrow lots of money; people copied his ideas; did not benefit from his invention	**WHEN** around 1439
	HOW developed a method of printing using individual metal letters
	WHY he wanted to find a way to make books more easily available

BACKGROUND	Before Gutenberg's printing press, books were written out by hand, usually in Latin. This made them extremely rare and expensive. Only universities and the richest people owned books.

INVENTION ❶

Built a revolutionary printing press so books were easier and cheaper to make.

Gutenberg

ACHIEVEMENT ❷

Changed the world by making books and information available to everybody.

INVENTION ❸

Developed an ink with linseed oil that dried quickly on paper.

NAME: Johannes Gutenberg
BORN: around 1398
DIED: age about 70
NATIONALITY: from the Electorate of Mainz
JOB: metalworker, printer
FAMOUS FOR: building a revolutionary printing press and printing the Gutenberg Bible

→ An early print workshop in action. An operator turns the handle of the press while his boss studies the material being printed.

THE FIRST PRINTING PRESS

⟫ How would Johannes Gutenberg change people's lives forever?

↑ The most famous book Gutenberg printed was the Gutenberg Bible. The text was in Latin and the decorations were handpainted. Only about 48 copies survive. They are among the most valuable books in the world.

⟫ HOW TO ...

Make a Potato Print
You will need: baking potato · cookie cutter · knife · fabric paint · paintbrush · card stock

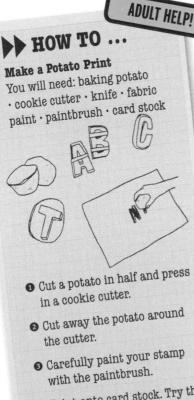

❶ Cut a potato in half and press in a cookie cutter.

❷ Cut away the potato around the cutter.

❸ Carefully paint your stamp with the paintbrush.

❹ Print onto card stock. Try this with alphabet cookie cutters to print like Gutenberg!

↑ A case full of metal type and numbers. The letters and numbers are back to front but they appear the right way round when printed onto paper.

Before Gutenberg built his printing press, few people could read or write. Most people passed their whole lives without ever setting eyes on a book. It was the Middle Ages and everyone in Europe lived in small, isolated villages. Information was passed on by word of mouth and news did not travel far. But after Gutenberg, that all changed.

Gutenberg came up with three brilliant ideas. First, he adapted a wine press, which is a machine that crushes grapes, to make a printing press. Secondly, he cast metal in molds to make hard-wearing individual letters, which could be used again and again. Thirdly, he developed a thick ink that would stick to the metal letters, dry quickly and not smudge on paper.

No one is sure exactly how Gutenberg's press worked. The printer probably spelled out a line of words on a rack like the one you use in a game of Scrabble. Then he lined up the racks on a big board to make a page. The board lay on the bed of the press and the printer spread ink over it, placed a damp sheet of paper on top and screwed down the heavy plate to print the words onto the paper.

The process became known as printing with movable type. A Chinese inventor, Bi Sheng, had already invented movable type around 1058 CE using clay letters, but they broke easily. Gutenberg improved the system. He could duplicate the same page quickly and many times over, which made books cheaper to produce. Gutenberg's life was not easy though. He borrowed money to develop his ideas and was sued by his business partner. He lost his business and ended up in debt. By the time he died, people had forgotten about him.

But Gutenberg's invention wasn't forgotten. By the early 1500s, over 1,000 print shops had sprung up in Europe and had started a revolution. Books were now printed in local languages instead of Latin and many people learned to read. Many books were about science, so knowledge about this subject grew. Religious beliefs changed too. As information spread, the all-powerful Catholic Church lost its grip and people began to follow other Christian religions. Gutenberg might have been shocked to discover all the changes he set into effect and also to learn that today many people think his printing press was the single most important invention of the last 1,000 years.

↑ This is a reconstruction of Gutenberg's printing press based on a screw wine press. On the bed of the press, you can see the roller for applying the ink.

EXTRA
STORY OF PRINTING

People have tried to print words onto cloth or paper since ancient times.

In China, printers carved words and pictures into wooden blocks, rolled ink onto them and stamped the blocks onto paper. This was called **block printing**. The Chinese invented this technique as early as the 7th century.

In 1844, about 400 years after Gutenberg's hand-operated press, printing went mechanical and became even faster. The **rotary press** fed a long roll of paper between two cylinders to print.

Today, people still buy printed books but they may also read **e-books** or find information online at the click of a mouse. Will we print books in the future? What do you think?

RACE TO INVENT THE TELEPHONE

THE BIG IDEA	≫ To make communication faster than ever before with a device that would let people talk to each other from different places.

CHALLENGES	**WHAT** **THE TELEPHONE**
	WHO Alexander Graham Bell and Elisha Gray
	WHERE Massachussetts and Illinois, United States
Other inventors trying to get there first; long and expensive battles in the courts	**WHEN** 1876
	HOW by transmitting, or sending, speech along an electrical wire
	WHY to pass on news and to do business more easily

BACKGROUND	Before the invention of the telephone, people communicated over long distances by telegraph. This was an electrical machine that sent a coded text message along a wire.

INVENTION ❶

Both Bell and Gray built telephones but Gray's device was not widely used.

ACHIEVEMENT ❷

Bell and Gray started companies that helped to make the telephone popular all over the world.

NAME: Alexander Graham Bell
BORN: March 3, 1847
DIED: age 75
NATIONALITY: Scottish
JOB: engineer, teacher
FAMOUS FOR: inventing the first practical telephone and teaching deaf people

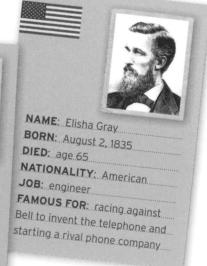

NAME: Elisha Gray
BORN: August 2, 1835
DIED: age 65
NATIONALITY: American
JOB: engineer
FAMOUS FOR: racing against Bell to invent the telephone and starting a rival phone company

→ Bell makes a telephone call for the opening of a long-distance phone line between New York and Chicago in 1892. His work as a teacher of deaf people inspired a lifelong interest in sound.

≫ Who would win the battle to be called the inventor of the telephone?

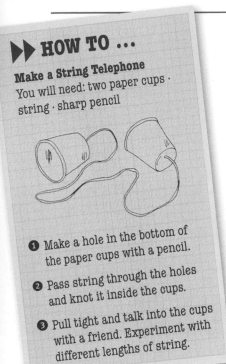

↑ An astonished audience watches and listens as Alexander Graham Bell demonstrates his new invention – the telephone.

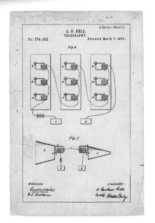

↑ This is one of the documents that Bell sent to the patent office.

While Alexander Graham Bell worked late into the night in one part of the United States, Elisha Gray did exactly the same thing in another – about 1,600 km (1,000 miles) away. Both were furiously developing a ground-breaking device that changed the human voice into electrical signals and sent it along a wire so that a person at the other end could hear the voice. It was the telephone.

Neither had perfected his machine before applying for a patent, which is a document from the government that protects an invention. If one of them got it, the invention would belong to him for a set amount of time. Nobody else would be able to copy his idea or make telephones and sell them without his permission.

SHARING THE PRIZE

Deciding who is the inventor of a device can be tricky. All of these talented scientists played a part in either inspiring the telephone or helping it to become a practical machine.

1854	1861	1865	1871
Charles Bourseul suggests that you can send sounds using electricity.	Johann Philipp Reis builds a device that sends speech but it is not clear. He calls it the 'telephon'.	A decription of Innocenzo Manzetti's 'speaking telegraph' appears in the newspapers.	Antonio Meucci tries to patent a telephone after years of building devices but runs out of money.

The two inventors drew up designs and explained how their machines worked. On February 14, 1876, Bell's lawyer rushed to the patent office to file Bell's documents. Gray hurried along to file his documents the same day. Bell's application was fifth in the list and Gray's was number 39. About three weeks later, on March 7, Bell got the patent.

But that wasn't the end of the story. Bell had not yet demonstrated a working telephone. When he did, it contained a part similar to one Gray had invented. Some people accused Bell of stealing Gray's idea! For years, battles raged about whether Bell deserved his patent, but each time the courts ruled in his favor. Winning the patent gave Bell the credit for the invention and it helped to make him a wealthy man. Gray continued inventing electrical equipment and ended up with many other patents to his name.

↑ Elisha Gray rushes to the patent office to block Bell's patent for the telephone. He was hoping to buy more time so that he could prove that his device was better.

← An early Bell telephone from 1877. Bell used this phone to demonstrate his invention to Queen Victoria in England.

'Mr Watson, come here, I want to see you.'
The first words heard clearly on a telephone, spoken by Bell.

↑ Telephones have come a long way since Bell's time. Today, billions of people own a mobile phone. We regularly upgrade and styles go out of date in the blink of an eye.

1876 (February)	1876 (March)	1876 (March)	1877	1877-78	1915
Bell's lawyer and Gray race to the patent office with their telephone designs.	Bell is given the patent for his telephone.	Bell transmits a clear message on a telephone to his assistant, Mr Watson, in the room next door.	Tivadar Puskás builds the first telephone exchange to connect more people to phones.	Thomas Edison invents a microphone that improves sound quality over longer distances.	Bell makes the first coast-to-coast phone call from New York to California, about 5,500 km (3,400 miles) away.

THE BIRTH OF THE MOVIES

THE BIG IDEA	» To create a magical machine that could film moving pictures and show them to an audience.
CHALLENGES Making still pictures move; the camera film was dangerous and could burst into flames	**WHAT** **CINÉMATOGRAPHE** **WHO** Louis and Auguste Lumière **WHERE** Lyon and Paris, France **WHEN** 1895 **HOW** by modifying existing devices **WHY** to bring clear, moving pictures to an audience
BACKGROUND	The brothers knew of other early movie equipment, including Thomas Edison's kinetoscope and Léon Bouly's version of the cinématographe. They knew they could do much better.

NAME: Louis Lumière
BORN: October 5, 1864
DIED: age 83
NATIONALITY: French
JOB: manufacturer, filmmaker
FAMOUS FOR: along with his brother, becoming one of the earliest filmmakers in history

INVENTION ①
Built the cinématographe, which combined a camera to make a film and a projector to show it.

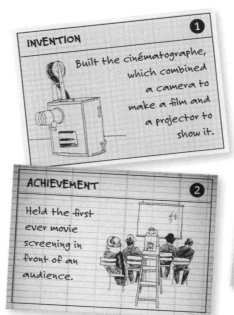

ACHIEVEMENT ②
Held the first ever movie screening in front of an audience.

NAME: Auguste Lumière
BORN: October 19, 1862
DIED: age 91
NATIONALITY: French
JOB: manufacturer, filmmaker
FAMOUS FOR: developing filmmaking equipment and making films with his brother

→ Louis Lumière studies a roll of celluloid film. This type of film was used by filmmakers in the early 20th century. If it got too hot, it would burst into flames. Fires at cinemas were common.

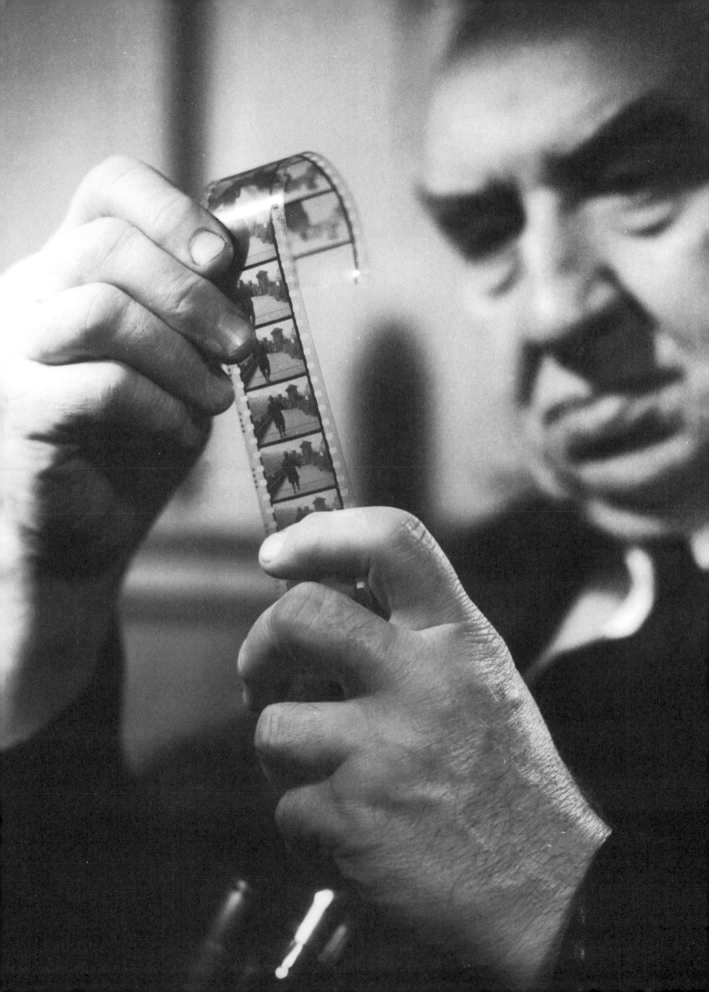

THE BIRTH OF THE MOVIES

>> How would the Lumière Brothers get their new invention to work properly?

peephole

↑ In 1891, Thomas Edison invented the kinetoscope. To view the moving pictures inside the box, you looked through a peephole and saw them magnified below.

↑ This is a still from the Lumière Brothers' first film. It's a short documentary known as *Leaving the Factory*. Many people believe this is the first proper movie ever made. If you'd like to see it, you can watch it for free on the Internet.

Louis Lumière was lying in bed with the flu when he came up with the solution to a problem that had been troubling him for months. It was December 1894. He and his brother, Auguste, were building a new type of camera. It could take lots of still pictures one after the other and play them back so quickly that they seemed to move. But the brothers couldn't figure out how best to run strips of film through the camera.

Suddenly Louis had a brainwave. He thought about how a sewing machine worked and it gave him an idea. He could adapt how a sewing machine stopped and started quickly so that his film would do the same. This would make the pictures look like they were moving while keeping them sharp and clear.

The brothers had seen an earlier movie-making machine called a kinetoscope. They were impressed but knew their invention was better. Their machine was smaller and lighter so it could be carried around for filming. It also had another huge advantage – the pictures could be projected so that several people could watch a movie at once. Only one person at a time could see a movie on a kinetoscope.

roll of film

magic lantern   cinématographe

→ A cinématographe with a magic lantern, which provides light so that the images will project clearly onto a wall or screen.

FROM PHOTOGRAPHY TO FILM
It was a huge leap from taking a still photograph to shooting moving pictures. There were many clever inventions and developments along the way.

around 1826	1878	1882	1887
Joseph Niépce takes the first still photograph on a coated metal plate but it soon fades.	Eadweard Muybridge sets up 24 cameras in a row and captures movement. He takes photos of a horse galloping.	Étienne-Jules Marey builds a camera shaped like a gun that can take 12 pictures every second.	Hannibal Goodwin develops celluloid film. It is strong and flexible, which makes it extremely useful.

↑ This is probably the first film poster ever made. It advertises a screening of the Lumière Brothers' movies.

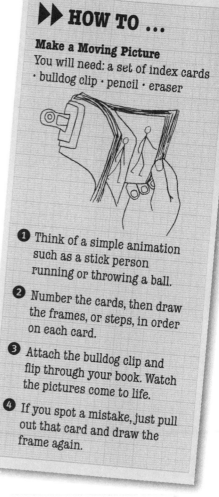

▶▶ HOW TO …

Make a Moving Picture
You will need: a set of index cards · bulldog clip · pencil · eraser

❶ Think of a simple animation such as a stick person running or throwing a ball.

❷ Number the cards, then draw the frames, or steps, in order on each card.

❸ Attach the bulldog clip and flip through your book. Watch the pictures come to life.

❹ If you spot a mistake, just pull out that card and draw the frame again.

In February 1895, Louis registered the invention so that no one else could copy it. He took the name 'cinématographe' from a similar but less effective machine made by Léon Bouly. It is where the word 'cinema' comes from.

The brothers started to make movies. They filmed workers leaving their father's factory, a comedy showing a gardener being sprayed with water by his own hose and people diving into a stormy sea. The movies were silent, in black and white and the longest one lasted for 49 seconds. On December 28, 1895, the brothers revealed their brilliant new invention to the world. They invited people to come and see ten of their short films in a dark room in a café in Paris. Thirty-three people turned up and paid one French franc each to watch the movies. The evening was an instant hit – the age of the cinema had begun.

↑ The Lumière Brothers made many groundbreaking films before returning to their real passion - inventing. One film, showing a train pulling into a station, seemed so real that it made the audience jump out of their seats!

1888	1889	1891	1892	1895 (February)	1895 (December)
Louis Le Prince builds a camera that captures the first moving images. Then he mysteriously disappears.	George Eastman improves celluloid film. He makes photography popular with the Kodak Brownie camera.	Thomas Edison invents the kinetoscope. One person can watch a movie through a peephole.	Léon Bouly registers a device called the cinématographe but can't afford the payments to keep the name.	The Lumière Brothers build their cinématographe.	People pay to go to the cinema for the first time and watch the Lumière Brothers' astonishing films.

RADIO ACROSS THE OCEAN

THE BIG IDEA	➤➤ To communicate over long distances with a system that could send and receive messages without wires.

CHALLENGES	
Working with poorly understood new technology; hugely expensive experiments	**WHAT** **RADIO TELEGRAPH** **WHO** Guglielmo Marconi **WHERE** England and Canada **WHEN** December 12, 1901 **HOW** by using radio waves that travel through the air **WHY** he wanted to build a successful communications business

BACKGROUND	Marconi first experimented with wireless devices at his home in Italy, making a bell ring in a different room. At the age of 21, he traveled to England and began to send long-distance messages.

INVENTION ①
Built a radio telegraph with a transmitter to send a message and a receiver to pick it up.

ACHIEVEMENT ②
Sent the first wireless message across the Atlantic Ocean.

ACHIEVEMENT ③
Formed a successful company that built and sold electronic devices for over 100 years.

NAME: Guglielmo Marconi
BORN: April 25, 1874
DIED: age 63
NATIONALITY: Italian
JOB: engineer, businessman
FAMOUS FOR: his work on wireless transmission and being one of the inventors of radio

→ Marconi built powerful transmitting stations on either side of the Atlantic Ocean to send messages to ships at sea. By the 1920s, his company dominated ship-to-shore communication.

WIRELESS
WORLD

MONTHLY 3D

RADIO ACROSS
THE OCEAN

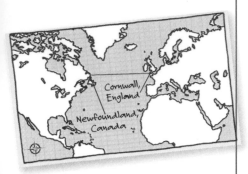

↑ Marconi's wireless message traveled from Cornwall in England to Newfoundland in Canada. It was a distance of about 3,500 km (2,175 miles).

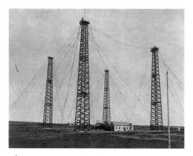

↑ The antennae that sent the signals were more than 60 meters (200 feet) high. That's about the same height as a 20-story building.

↑ A ship's officer sends a radio telegraph message. Marconi's company provided the service, the equipment and the operator.

These days with wireless hotspots and the Internet, we take it for granted that we can communicate instantly with people on the other side of the world. But in the early 1900s it was a trickier business. People were just starting to use telephones regularly and they sent urgent messages overseas by electric telegraph. An operator at one end tapped out a code, then someone else at the other end translated the signals into letters to make sentences. The electric telegraph needed wires to send information and engineers laid long cables under the sea.

In 1901, Marconi began one of his most ambitious projects – to send a message across the Atlantic Ocean by radio telegraph using radio waves and no cables. If it worked, it would be an astonishing leap forward for technology.

Marconi didn't discover radio waves. A Scottish scientist, James Clerk Maxwell, worked out that they existed in 1865. Then a German scientist, Heinrich Hertz, showed radio waves in action about 20 years later. Marconi read about this. He experimented with how far radio waves could travel and built a successful communications business out of them.

↑ Marconi with his radio telegraph equipment.

DANGER! In the winter, temperatures in Newfoundland can be as low as -13°F. Storms and high winds regularly batter the icy coastline.

↑ This is Signal Hill in Newfoundland where Marconi first received his wireless message from across the Atlantic Ocean.

At the transmitting station in Cornwall, Marconi set up 20 towering masts, but they blew down in a storm. He quickly built new ones. Then, Marconi set sail for Newfoundland, Canada. At the receiving station, it was more basic. He had kites and balloons to hold up a 155-meter-long (508-foot) wire in the air. In Newfoundland the winters are harsh. In the strong winds, the wire kept blowing away. Finally, around noon on December 12, Marconi heard the first of three clicks on his radio telegraph. The clicks were the code for the letter 'S', the message the operator had agreed to send.

Some doubted whether Marconi really did receive a message that day among the crackles. So in February 1902 he sent a ship across the ocean to record daily signals from the Cornwall station. Then on January 18, 1903, King Edward VII of England received a telegraph greeting from Theodore Roosevelt, the President of the United States. The age of wireless communication had begun.

← In later years, Marconi became involved in broadcast radio. His company built and sold many radios when they became a popular form of entertainment.

EXPERIMENTS IN TELEVISION

THE BIG IDEA	» To beam live pictures to a receiver, or TV set, bringing news and entertainment into people's homes.
CHALLENGES Suffered from poor health; some people didn't think television would catch on	**WHAT** TELEVISION **WHO** John Logie Baird **WHERE** London, England **WHEN** January 1926 **HOW** by 'scanning' light and turning it into an electrical signal **WHY** to find an invention he could make into a business
BACKGROUND	In the 1920s, people could watch movies at the cinema but most of them were silent. Some people had radios at home to listen to, or they read books and played board games.

INVENTION 1
Built the first working TV set and brought TV into people's homes.

ACHIEVEMENT 2
Led the way in making people believe in the future of TV.

INVENTION 3
Developed color television and also a TV for viewing in 3D.

NAME: John Logie Baird
BORN: August 13, 1888
DIED: age 57
NATIONALITY: Scottish
JOB: inventor, businessman
FAMOUS FOR: broadcasting the first moving pictures and bringing television to the nation

→ By the 1950s, televisions were a must-have luxury item. This ad appeared in a magazine of the time, tempting people to buy one.

MEDWAY
CORRUGATED CASE

>> Could Baird's weird-looking machine really send moving pictures?

↑ The early pictures Baird transmitted were of this ventriloquist's dummy. He called it 'Stooky Bill'.

↑ The first TV magazine came out in 1926. This edition from 1928 gave instructions on how to build your own TV.

↑ In 1936, the first public TV broadcasts were made from this transmitter at Alexandra Palace in London.

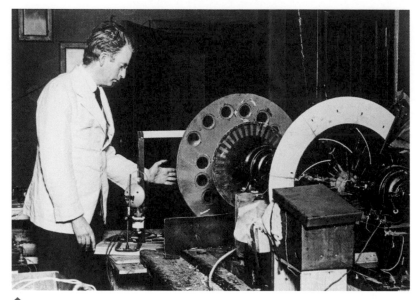

↑ Baird shows how his device works. Two large spinning discs with holes in them scanned light in lines to send a live image from one place to another.

Back in 1925, some people thought John Logie Baird was mad when he told them that he'd found a way to transmit live pictures and had built a receiver so that you could see them. An editor of a national newspaper even tried to get rid of Baird when he showed up at the newspaper offices looking for a way to promote his weird new machine. It's true that Baird had come up with a few curious inventions, including a glass razor that wouldn't rust but broke easily while shaving and a pair of air-cushioned shoes with balloons in their soles that kept on bursting. But television wasn't one of them. This was the work of a genius!

Baird started carrying out experiments in a workshop on the south coast of England. His first machine included a hat box, bicycle lights and sewing needles. When he moved to London, he managed to transmit pictures of objects that appeared as black-and-white shadows. He held a demonstration in a department store. But there was still more work to do.

'Go down to reception and get rid of a lunatic who is there. He says he's got a machine for seeing by wireless!'
A newspaper editor, talking about Baird

DANGER! While experimenting, Baird got electric shocks, his equipment jumped about and sometimes the spinning discs exploded!

Baird had to make the pictures clearer. He carried out tests with a ventriloquist's dummy. Getting nowhere and running out of money, he felt like giving up. But then, on October 2, 1925, he saw the dummy's head appear in detail on a tiny screen. Excitedly, he rushed downstairs and grabbed an office boy called William Taynton who became the first person to appear live on TV. On January 26, 1926, Baird demonstrated his invention again. This time he transmitted the image of a person. The picture was blurry but you could see the person's mouth move.

Baird didn't invent television alone. He developed his ideas and those of other scientists to make a working machine. Through his passion and drive he brought television to people's attention and made them believe it was a useful invention. Nearly 100 years later, there is a TV set in most people's homes. Perhaps the 'madman' was right after all!

↑ Today, TV works differently from Baird's time. We watch digital pictures and, for many of us, a satellite in space beams those pictures to our TV sets.

EXTRA

CHANGING STYLES

In the early days, only rich people could afford to buy television sets.

In 1929, this was one of the first models to go on sale. It was extremely expensive and only about 20 were made. Baird called his machines '**televisors**'.

This **tin box televisor** came out in the 1930s. It was cheaper than the wooden model above but still cost nearly $4,700 in today's money.

In 1936, Baird launched a **color TV**. Inside, it had a device called a cathode ray tube to make it work. Color TV was a luxury item that only a few people could afford.

CODES AND COMPUTER SCIENCE

THE BIG IDEA	»» To design a machine that could crack a fiendishly complicated wartime code.
CHALLENGES Worked during wartime; code kept changing; the UK government mistreated Turing	**WHAT BOMBE MACHINE** **WHO** Alan Turing **WHERE** Bletchley Park, Buckinghamshire, England **WHEN** 1939 to 1945 **HOW** with complex mathematics and original thinking **WHY** to discover the secret plans of the German Armed Forces
BACKGROUND	During World War II (1939–1945), the German Army, Navy and Air Force sent secret messages to one another using the Enigma Code. The Allies needed to break the code to learn their enemy's plans.

INVENTION ❶
Devised the ingenious Bombe machine for breaking an enemy code.

ACHIEVEMENT ❷
Is likely to have shortened the length of World War II, saving millions of people's lives.

INVENTION ❸
Designed the Automatic Computing Engine (ACE), which was one of the first proper computers.

NAME: Alan Turing
BORN: June 23, 1912
DIED: age 41
NATIONALITY: English
JOB: mathematician
FAMOUS FOR: breaking the Enigma Code and his ground-breaking work on computers

→ Engineers built over 200 Bombe machines at Bletchley Park. After World War II, they were all destroyed. In 2007, a new Bombe machine was made to show visitors to Bletchley Park how it worked.

⟫ How would Turing's secret mission help to win World War II?

On September 4, 1939, a few days after the start of World War II, Alan Turing reported for duty at the Government Code and Cypher School in Bletchley Park, England. The government asked him to find a way to read the coded messages that the German Armed Forces were sending to one another using the Enigma Code. His mission was top secret. To his bosses, the task seemed impossible. Not only was the code one of the most complicated ever made, the Germans kept changing it. There were over 150 trillion ways that it could be set up. But for Turing this was exactly the kind of mathematical challenge he could get his teeth into.

In a short space of time, Turing designed a machine called the Bombe. Its job was to discover the Enigma Code settings for the day by ruling out the wrong possibilities. An operator ran the noisy machine at night, watching it stop, start and calculate. It may have got its name because it made alarming ticking noises that sounded like an unexploded bomb.

Once the Bombe had discovered the setttings, operators could then decode individual messages. Sometimes the messages said nothing much, but other times they revealed important plans. The German Armed Forces had no idea that their code had been broken.

→ The Germans created their code on an Enigma Machine.

↑ The inside of a Bombe machine was extremely complicated. It was filled with hundreds of connectors and at least 19 km (12 miles) of wire. In today's money, one machine cost about $800,000 to build.

rotors changed every day to set new code

coded letters light up on lampboard

operator types on keyboard

plugboard makes code trickier

↑ At the height of the war, there were over 9,000 staff working at Bletchley Park. Nearly all of them were women.

↑ After leaving Bletchley Park, Turing built the Automatic Computing Engine, or ACE computer. It was one of the earliest machines that could store instructions in its memory.

During World War II, a battle raged in the Atlantic Ocean. German submarines, called U-boats, tried to stop ships from North America bringing troops, equipment and food to Great Britain. With the help of Turing's Bombe machines, operators discovered the U-boat plans of attack, so many ships got through. The Allied Forces, which included Britain, Russia and the United States, won the Battle of the Atlantic and soon the war itself.

For over 30 years, Turing's work remained a closely guarded secret. He went on to develop the first computers, but he sadly died at a young age in 1954. He had been treated very badly by the UK government and his work was not fully recognized. During the 1970s, information about Bletchley Park came to light and people realized the huge role Turing played in saving many people's lives. Today, he is celebrated around the world as both a war hero and a computing genius.

← Turing had a few eccentric habits. He chained his cup to a radiator so that it wouldn't get stolen and he refused to fix his bicycle even though the chain kept falling off.

↑ Turing wrote about machines 'thinking' like humans long before anyone else. Today, we call this artificial intelligence or AI. ASIMO, produced by Honda, is one of the world's most advanced humanoid AI robots who can learn new things, 'see', speak and perform tasks.

THE ARRIVAL OF THE INTERNET

THE BIG IDEA	» A new way to communicate – to let people see and share information on any computer, anywhere in the world.
CHALLENGES Keeping the Web a free, fair and safe space for everybody to use and enjoy	**WHAT WORLDWIDE WEB** **WHO** Tim Berners-Lee **WHERE** England **WHEN** 1991 **HOW** by thinking big and connecting lots of ideas **WHY** he hopes it will help people to understand each other better
BACKGROUND	The World Wide Web is part of the Internet. In the 1960s, computer scientists in the United States created a small network of computers called ARPANET. It inspired the Internet that we know today.

INVENTION ❶
Developed a system that connected information and let people share web pages.

ACHIEVEMENT ❷
Helped to make the Internet a huge part of our daily lives.

INVENTION ❸
Came up with the name World Wide Web (www.), which is used in all website addresses today.
http://www

NAME: Tim Berners-Lee
BORN: June 8, 1955
NATIONALITY: English
JOB: computer scientist
FAMOUS FOR: inventing the World Wide Web and building the first website and web browser to find information on the Web

→ From an early age, Tim Berners-Lee was interested in mathematics and electronics. As a schoolboy, he built electronic devices to control his model trains. He also loved science fiction stories.

THE ARRIVAL OF
THE INTERNET

≫ How did Tim Berners-Lee's visionary work change all of our daily lives?

When you want to find out a piece of information, what do you do? It's likely that you head straight to a computer or grab a smartphone and search on the Internet. The information pops up in seconds. The brilliant computer scientist who helped to make this possible is Tim Berners-Lee, inventor of the World Wide Web.

Today, we often use the words 'World Wide Web' and 'Internet' to mean the same thing, but they are different. The World Wide Web is all the linked documents, sounds and videos on websites. The Internet is the huge network of computers all over the world that we use to find and share information on the Web.

In 1990, Tim Berners-Lee worked in a laboratory in Europe called CERN. Today, this is where the Large Hadron Collider smashes tiny particles together to find out about the universe. Scientists come from all over the world to research there. Back then, Berners-Lee discovered an annoying problem. Many of the computers had different software, so it was very difficult for the scientists to share their work.

↑ As a student, Tim Berners-Lee built a computer out of an old TV. This is the computer he used at work to devise the World Wide Web.

▶▶ HOW ...

A Web Browser Works

❶ When you type in the web address, your web browser finds the computer that hosts, or stores, the website. It could be anywhere in the world!

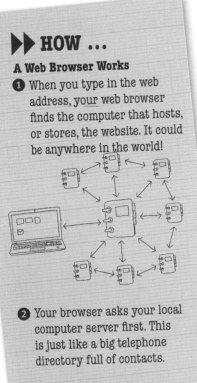

❷ Your browser asks your local computer server first. This is just like a big telephone directory full of contacts.

❸ These contacts ask more contacts until one finds the website and pings it back to you the way you found it. It all happens in a few seconds or less.

↑ There are many computer programming languages, but all are based on binary code. Combinations of just two numbers, 0 and 1, tell a computer what to do.

↑ At the 2012 Olympics opening ceremony in London, Tim Berners-Lee appeared inside a model house. He tweeted from his computer, 'This is for everyone'.

Frustrated by this, he came up with the idea for a system that would link the information together so that everyone at CERN could see it. Then, as he worked on his project, it dawned on him that he could do something much bigger. His system could reach the whole world, not just the people at CERN. It could be a World Wide Web. Initially, Berners-Lee had a different name for it – Information Mesh. But he was worried that it sounded too much like Information 'Mess'.

In December 1990, Tim Berners-Lee created the first web browser. In August 1991, he put it on the Internet. Berners-Lee also provided a website, which explained the browser and showed how to use it. Many inventions are built and sold to make money, but the World Wide Web was free for everyone to develop. It grew at a lightning pace. Today, through the World Wide Web, we can learn things, play games, shop, stay in touch with friends and share our ideas. It has changed our daily lives and is one of the most powerful ways in the world for us to communicate with each other.

← Google is one of the largest companies that provides services for the Internet. In 2012, it let people look at its top-secret data centers for the first time.

A REVOLUTION IN STEAM POWER

THE BIG IDEA	» To improve a clanking wasteful engine and turn it into something more efficient to power all kinds of machines.

CHALLENGES	WHAT **STEAM ENGINE**
	WHO James Watt
Hugely expensive to develop enormous machines driven by steam; often in poor health	WHERE Glasgow, Scotland and Birmingham, England
	WHEN 1765 to 1790
	HOW Watt was an excellent problem-solver and would not give up
	WHY he had a thirst for new technology and problem-solving

BACKGROUND	Around 1712, Thomas Newcomen built the first practical steam engine. By the mid 1700s, hundreds of his machines were used to pump water from mines, but they were slow and often broke down.

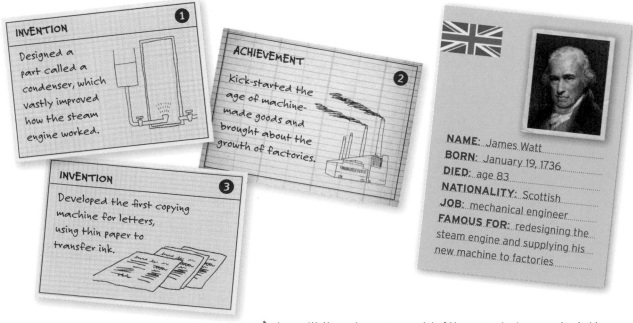

INVENTION ①
Designed a part called a condenser, which vastly improved how the steam engine worked.

ACHIEVEMENT ②
Kick-started the age of machine-made goods and brought about the growth of factories.

INVENTION ③
Developed the first copying machine for letters, using thin paper to transfer ink.

NAME: James Watt
BORN: January 19, 1736
DIED: age 83
NATIONALITY: Scottish
JOB: mechanical engineer
FAMOUS FOR: redesigning the steam engine and supplying his new machine to factories

→ James Watt puzzles over a model of Newcomen's steam engine in his workshop at Glasgow University. Watt started working for the university in his early twenties, building and repairing scientific instruments.

A REVOLUTION IN STEAM POWER

⟫ Watt was determined to perfect his engine. He needed to think harder ...

↑ Watt's first engines only produced up-and-down movement to power pumps. But his later engines, like this one, drove a wheel to power all kinds of industrial machines.

In 1763, a model of Newcomen's steam engine arrived at James Watt's workshop for repair. Watt worked at Glasgow University, where lecturers used the engine to explain the new technology of steam power to students. But it broke down frequently. Intrigued, Watt began to study Newcomen's engine in detail. It heated water to make steam, which in turn powered a pump. The steam entered a cylinder and pushed up a piston, or disc, to operate the pump. The steam was then cooled inside the cylinder and the piston went down. Watt realized the engine wasted a lot of heat. Could he improve it?

For two years, Watt slaved over the problem. Then one day, after a walk on Glasgow Green, the solution hit him. He would add a separate cylinder, or condenser, where the steam could cool. The main cylinder could stay hot all the time and keep working. It was a stroke of genius!

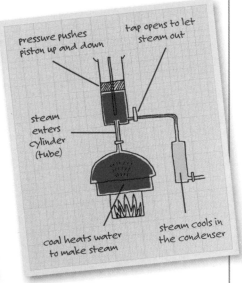

pressure pushes piston up and down

tap opens to let steam out

steam enters cylinder (tube)

coal heats water to make steam

steam cools in the condenser

↑ This is how Watt's steam engine worked with a separate condenser.

↑ When Watt died, the workshop in his attic was sealed. Over 50 years later, it was shipped off to the Science Museum in London, where you can still see it today.

FROM STEAM ENGINE TO STEAM TRAIN
This timeline charts the development of the steam engine during a time of great change called the Industrial Revolution. It played a vital part in the growth of a new kind of transport – the steam train.

1712	1765	1775	1784
Thomas Newcomen invents the first practical steam engine.	James Watt adds a condenser to make the engine much more effective.	Watt and Boulton go into business and start to build Watt's engine.	William Murdoch, who works for Watt, shows him a steam engine on wheels but Watt thinks it unsafe.

↑ This beam engine supplied air for an ironworks furnace in the West Midlands, England. Today, it stands as a monument to Watt's and Boulton's achievements.

↑ Watt and Boulton were successful business partners for over 25 years. Details of how their steam engines worked were kept secret.

Watt's hard work paid off. In 1775, he went into business with a factory owner called Matthew Boulton. They began to make and sell this new, more powerful steam engine. At first it was used to pump water out of coal, tin and copper mines. Then, as Watt improved the engine further, it began to power cotton mills and machines for weaving and spinning cloth.

Before Watt's steam engine, most goods were crafted by hand. Now they could be made by machine, much more quickly. Factories sprang up all over the country. By the time Watt died in 1819, there were 18 steam-powered weaving factories in Glasgow alone, with nearly 3,000 looms to make cloth. This change in Great Britain soon swept across the rest of the world. The age of industry and mass production took hold.

↑ The first steam engines were huge. But by the early 1800s, they had become small enough to be put on wheels and pull wagons as part of a train.

1788	1801	1804	1825	1828	1830
Watt improves his engine so that it can power machines as well as pumps.	Oliver Evans develops a smaller engine and says people will soon travel by steam train.	Richard Trevithick runs a steam locomotive along a track.	The first steam railway opens in the north of England. It carries coal from mines.	The steam train arrives in the United States, with the building of the Baltimore and Ohio Railroad.	The first steam passenger service starts in the north of England, then spreads worldwide.

LIGHTING UP THE WORLD

THE BIG IDEA	» To bring electric lighting into people's homes with an efficient light bulb.
CHALLENGES None – Edison saw every failed experiment as a step towards success	**WHAT** **PRACTICAL LIGHT BULB** **WHO** Thomas Edison **WHERE** Menlo Park, New Jersey, United States **WHEN** December 31, 1879 **HOW** he researched and experimented until something worked **WHY** Edison wanted to build a business out of inventing things
BACKGROUND	Several scientists developed the light bulb before Edison, including the English inventor, Joseph Swan. But Edison delivered lighting to people on a much bigger scale.

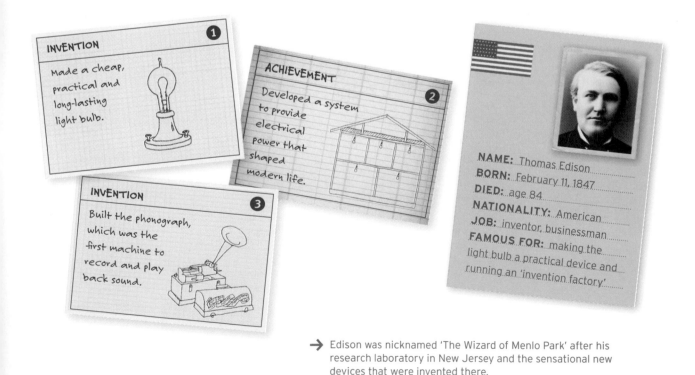

INVENTION 1
Made a cheap, practical and long-lasting light bulb.

ACHIEVEMENT 2
Developed a system to provide electrical power that shaped modern life.

INVENTION 3
Built the phonograph, which was the first machine to record and play back sound.

NAME: Thomas Edison
BORN: February 11, 1847
DIED: age 84
NATIONALITY: American
JOB: inventor, businessman
FAMOUS FOR: making the light bulb a practical device and running an 'invention factory'

→ Edison was nicknamed 'The Wizard of Menlo Park' after his research laboratory in New Jersey and the sensational new devices that were invented there.

LIGHTING UP
THE WORLD

≫ What would the Wizard of Menlo Park invent next?

By the time Thomas Edison lit up a street in Menlo Park, New Jersey with his new, soft-glow electric lighting, he was already well on the way to becoming a world-famous inventor. It was New Year's Eve, 1879, and around 3,000 people arrived in specially arranged trains to see the dazzling display. It seemed that Edison had come up with another miracle. In reality, it had taken a lot of time and hard work.

For over a year, Edison and his lab assistants had experimented with the filament, or thread, inside a traditional light bulb. They were looking for something that would glow for a long time and was cheap to make. Over 1,000 materials were tried, including coconut fibers, fishing line and even hairs from a person's beard! Edison and his team worked through the night, snacking and cat-napping along the way.

Eventually, Edison decided to bake a cotton thread, which turned it into carbon. When the carbonized thread was tested in a light bulb, it glowed for 40 hours. Impressed by the result, Edison experimented with other plant fibers until he discovered that carbonized bamboo worked best. Before long, he had made a light bulb that glowed for 1,200 hours.

↑ This is an Edison lamp. An electric current passed through the carbon thread inside the bulb to make it glow. Before electric lighting, people used gas lamps at home, which flickered and had a dangerous flame.

Edison said
'Genius is one per cent inspiration, ninety-nine per cent perspiration.'

↑ Lewis Latimer was an engineer, and part of Edison's brilliant team. His work on the carbon filament was vital to the success of Edison's light bulb. He also drew up the plans for Alexander Graham Bell's telephone.

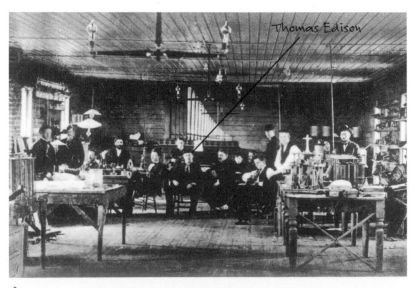

Thomas Edison

↑ Edison sits in his lab surrounded by his assistants. He played the pipe organ from time to time to give them breaks during late-night shifts.

For a publicity stunt in New York, Edison staged a late-night parade. Four hundred men marched through the streets wearing light bulbs on their heads!

But this was only the start of Edison's grand plan. To put lighting into people's homes, he had to provide all the equipment and find an effective way to supply electrical power, too. So, his team designed lamps, sockets and switches. They built power stations and generators, and laid all the wires to get electricity into people's houses. Edison's power stations provided electricity for businesses and factories. He transformed people's lives at home and at work.

Edison researched and experimented for his whole life. He registered over 1,000 different inventions. But he will perhaps be best remembered for his light bulb. When he died in 1931, to honor his achievements, people all over the United States held a one-minute silence with all the lights switched off.

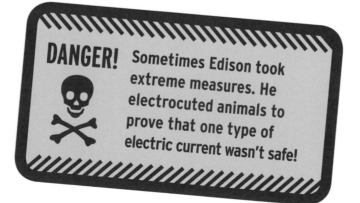

DANGER! Sometimes Edison took extreme measures. He electrocuted animals to prove that one type of electric current wasn't safe!

EXTRA

INVENTION FACTORY

Edison churned out one device after another.

In 1877, he caused a sensation by inventing the **phonograph**, which made the first clear recording of a human voice. Soon, people were buying phonographs to play their favorite songs.

He also designed the **kinetograph**, one of the first cameras to film movies, and built an early cinema projector. He often improved existing inventions as well as buying ideas from other people.

Some of his more unusual devices included an **electric duplicating ink pen**, which later inspired the tattoo needle, and a ghost-detecting machine. No one is sure if he built his ghost detector!

⏻ THE INCREDIBLE TESLA COIL

THE BIG IDEA	➤➤ To send powerful bolts of electricity through the air and the ground without any wires.

CHALLENGES	
Expensive projects and experiments; some saw Tesla's ideas as crazy and unrealistic	**WHAT** TESLA COIL **WHO** Nikola Tesla **WHERE** Colorado and New York, United States **WHEN** 1899 to 1905 **HOW** Tesla pictured inventions in his head, then built them **WHY** he wanted to power the world wirelessly

BACKGROUND	In 1884, Tesla traveled from Europe to the United States to work for Thomas Edison (see pages 58 to 61). But after a falling-out, he left the job to develop his own ideas about electricity, energy and power.

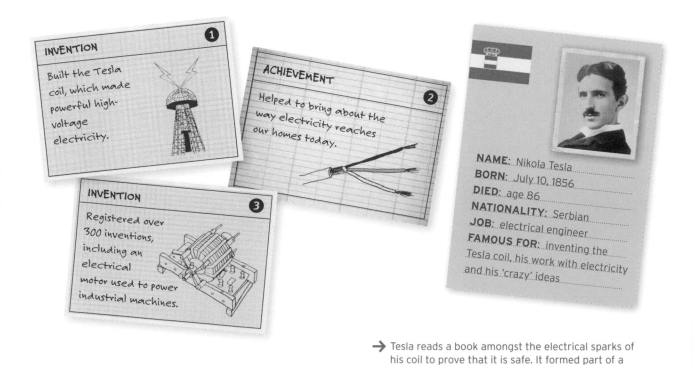

INVENTION ❶

Built the Tesla coil, which made powerful high-voltage electricity.

ACHIEVEMENT ❷

Helped to bring about the way electricity reaches our homes today.

INVENTION ❸

Registered over 300 inventions, including an electrical motor used to power industrial machines.

NAME: Nikola Tesla
BORN: July 10, 1856
DIED: age 86
NATIONALITY: Serbian
JOB: electrical engineer
FAMOUS FOR: inventing the Tesla coil, his work with electricity and his 'crazy' ideas

→ Tesla reads a book amongst the electrical sparks of his coil to prove that it is safe. It formed part of a giant transmitting station in his lab in Colorado, USA.

THE INCREDIBLE
TESLA COIL

» Would Tesla's outlandish and ambitious electrical experiment work?

When Nikola Tesla moved his lab to Colorado in 1899, he had big plans. He'd already developed an amazing device, which would become known as the Tesla coil. It could produce bolts of powerful high-voltage electricity without any wires. At Colorado Springs, he built a giant version of this device and called it a magnifying transmitter. Tesla told the newspapers that he was carrying out experiments in sending wireless messages. But he had another mission, too. Tesla wanted to transmit electricity through the air to power lights and machinery. He saw a future where the whole world was powered in this way. He believed that the magnifying transmitter would be his greatest invention.

One evening, Tesla tested his machine. Bolts of electricity shot out of the tower above the lab and light bulbs outside began to glow. In a nearby town, people saw sparks jump between their feet and heard a noise like the rumble of thunder. Then the whole town went dark. Tesla's experiment had burnt out the power station! The local people were terrified, but Tesla thought it was a great success.

↑ Our homes are powered by alternating current (AC). Powerful high-voltage electricity is made at a power station, then brought down to a safe level before it arrives in our homes. Tesla was one of the first people to develop this system.

The scientific man does not aim at an immediate result ... his duty is to lay the foundation for those who are to come, and point the way.'
Nikola Tesla

↑ Tesla helped to develop the first hydroelectric power station at Niagara Falls, using the power of falling water to make electricity. Today, power stations at Niagara supply electricity to thousands of homes in Canada and the USA.

↑ Tesla's towering New York transmitter had a 57-meter (187-foot) -high wooden frame with a steel dome on top. The Tesla coil was inside the wooden frame.

↑ Today, Tesla coils are mainly used for entertainment. Here, 1 million volts of electricity from seven Tesla coils stream around the magician David Blaine.

Determined to continue, Tesla began to build a bigger transmitter in New York. He convinced businessmen to give him money for the project, telling them that he was developing a worldwide communication system. Then in 1901, Marconi (see pages 38 to 41) sent the first wireless message across the Atlantic Ocean. Marconi used lots of Tesla's ideas, but for Tesla it was too late. His backers pulled out and by 1905 his plans had fallen apart. Today, we know that Tesla could have easily sent a wireless message from his towering transmitter, but his dream of providing electrical power wirelessly on a large scale would not have worked.

In old age, Tesla fell into poverty and people began to see him as a 'mad scientist'. But now, more than 70 years after his death, scientists remember Tesla's achievements. As well as developing wireless transmission, his work on alternating electrical current plays a large part in how electricity reaches our homes today. Perhaps as importantly, his futuristic ideas dare modern-day inventors to think big.

← Tesla had numerous obsessions, including a love of pigeons. He took them home to live with him if they looked weak or ill.

EXTRA

AHEAD OF THE GAME

Tesla worked on many new inventions but he was bad at business and making them successful.

In 1898, he amazed an audience with a **remote-controlled** boat. Today, everyone uses a remote control for TV at home.

Around 1894, while experimenting with the Tesla coil, he may have taken one of the earliest **x-ray photographs.** Other scientists went onto develop x-rays further.

The Tesla coil also led him to develop some of the first **fluorescent and neon lights.**

MANUFACTURING
KEVLAR

THE BIG IDEA	>> To create a super-strong yet lightweight material to replace the heavy steel cord in car tires.

CHALLENGES	
Other scientists unwilling to trust her ideas; women chemists not recognized	**WHAT** KEVLAR® **WHO** Stephanie Kwolek **WHERE** DuPont laboratory, Delaware, United States **WHEN** 1964 **HOW** Kwolek made a liquid with chemicals, then spun it into a fiber **WHY** she relished the challenge and loved making new discoveries

BACKGROUND	Kwolek was very interested in fashion. When she went to work for DuPont, a large chemical company, they had already invented the human-made fiber, nylon, which we find in sweaters today.

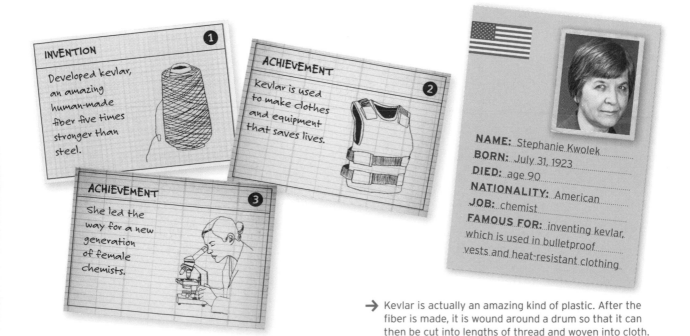

INVENTION ❶
Developed kevlar, an amazing human-made fiber five times stronger than steel.

ACHIEVEMENT ❷
Kevlar is used to make clothes and equipment that saves lives.

ACHIEVEMENT ❸
She led the way for a new generation of female chemists.

NAME: Stephanie Kwolek
BORN: July 31, 1923
DIED: age 90
NATIONALITY: American
JOB: chemist
FAMOUS FOR: inventing kevlar, which is used in bulletproof vests and heat-resistant clothing.

→ Kevlar is actually an amazing kind of plastic. After the fiber is made, it is wound around a drum so that it can then be cut into lengths of thread and woven into cloth.

MANUFACTURING
KEVLAR

⟫ Was there more to the liquid in Kwolek's test tube than met the eye?

↑ Kwolek holds up a test tube filled with the murky liquid from which she made kevlar. The gloves she is wearing contain kevlar fibers. In its natural state, kevlar is yellow in color, but sometimes it is dyed.

↑ This is what kevlar cloth looks like close up. There are different types. Kevlar-29 cloth is soft and suitable for clothing. Often kevlar fibers are combined with other kinds of fibers.

↑ The best-known use of kevlar is for life-saving body armor and bulletproof vests. But you might also discover kevlar in your cell phone case or high-tech sneakers!

After leaving college in her early twenties, Stephanie Kwolek took a job in a research laboratory for a company called DuPont. She was one of only a handful of female chemists employed by the company at the time. Her plan was to earn enough money to train to become a doctor. But Kwolek soon realized that she found the job really satisfying. It gave her the chance to do things she loved – experimenting, being creative and making discoveries – so she decided to stay. In 1965, the bosses at DuPont set Kwolek and the other chemists a challenge.

The world was facing a gas shortage. A lightweight yet super-strong material was needed to replace the heavy steel cord used inside car tires. Then tires would weigh less and cars could run more efficiently, using less gas. Kwolek got to work. During one of her experiments, she made a peculiar watery and cloudy liquid. She was aiming to produce a thick, clear liquid that was easy to work with. This looked like a mistake. Many scientists would have thrown the liquid away, but Kwolek was curious and wanted to investigate further.

↑ When dealing with high-temperature fires, firefighters often wear heat-resistant suits containing kevlar so they can get close enough to the blaze to put it out.

This astronaut tests out a flexible yet super-tough space suit in Antarctica for future space travel. It is made from over 350 materials, including kevlar.

The next step was to spin the liquid in a machine called a spinneret to turn it into a fiber. The process was similar to how you spin liquid sugar to make candy floss. She asked another scientist to do the job but he was worried that Kwolek's strange liquid contained tiny solid particles that would plug up and damage his machine. Eventually she persuaded him to give it a go. To their amazement, the liquid spun beautifully. Not only that, the fiber they made from it was light, flexible and five times stronger than steel! It also didn't become hot easily.

A dancer performs with her fire rope in the dark. The rope has a slow-burning kevlar wick at the end so she can create an exciting display when it is set on fire.

DuPont named the fiber kevlar and began to develop ways to use it. As well as car tires, kevlar was soon strengthening all kinds of products from tennis rackets, skis and other sports equipment to work gloves, safety helmets and even space suits. Its fire-resistant qualities and super-strength made it a life-saving material. Kwolek worked for DuPont for 40 years. By the time she retired, she had received countless awards and become a member of the United States National Inventors Hall of Fame. Kwolek is one of too few famous female inventors and she remains an inspiration to women around the world.

A racing-car body is usually a blend of kevlar and carbon fiber. This makes the car lightweight enough to travel at speed and the cockpit strong enough to protect the driver in an accident.

BIRTH OF THE MOTOR CAR

## THE BIG IDEA	» To build a wheeled vehicle powered by an engine that people could drive along a road – the first motor car.
## CHALLENGES Competition from other inventors; danger of crashes; risk of money running out	**WHAT** **BENZ PATENT MOTORWAGON** **WHO** Karl Benz and his wife, Bertha Benz **WHERE** Mannheim, Germany **WHEN** 1885 to 1888 **HOW** Karl invented the motor car; Bertha showed its practical use **WHY** to develop a new type of long-distance transport
## BACKGROUND	Before the motor car, people traveled from town to town in horse-drawn carriages called stagecoaches, and later by steam train. In cities, the horse-drawn bus was a popular way to get around.

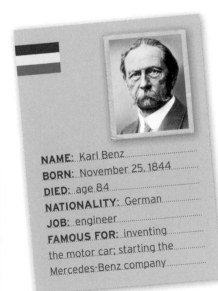

NAME: Karl Benz
BORN: November 25, 1844
DIED: age 84
NATIONALITY: German
JOB: engineer
FAMOUS FOR: inventing the motor car; starting the Mercedes-Benz company

INVENTION ❶

Karl invented a practical motor car. It contained an engine that burned fuel.

ACHIEVEMENT ❷

Bertha made a 212-km (131-mile) round trip in Karl's motor car, proving it was suitable for long-distance travel.

NAME: Bertha Benz
BORN: May 3, 1849
DIED: age 95
NATIONALITY: German
JOB: businesswoman
FAMOUS FOR: showing the value of the motor car; starting the Mercedes-Benz company

→ A scene from a film made to celebrate the 100-year anniversary of Bertha Benz's daredevil road trip. Here, Bertha sets off with help from her sons.

BIRTH OF THE
MOTOR CAR

▶▶ Could Bertha show Karl that his new invention was world-changing?

In 1885, Karl Benz showed his wife, Bertha, a brand-new type of vehicle. It ran on wheels and moved by itself, powered by a gas engine. It was a motor car. Karl's genius invention hadn't come about overnight. For a long time, he'd worked on how to keep the engine cool and had experimented with different fuels. He'd also developed a starting mechanism and a way to control the car's speed. Benz continued to improve the vehicle and show his wife each new model.

By 1888, Bertha Benz was growing frustrated. She knew Karl was a brilliant inventor, but he was no businessman. He'd only marketed the car as a curiosity – a toy for adults. She decided to take matters into her own hands. Bertha had helped out her husband before, using her own money to support his first company when it failed. Early one morning in August, she crept downstairs with her two teenage sons and left a note for her husband on the table. She said that she was taking the boys to see her mother in a town called Pforzheim, over 106 km (66 miles) away. What she didn't say was that she planned to use Karl's car and show the world exactly what his fabulous new vehicle could do.

↑ An ad for the Benz Patent Motorwagen. Between 1885 and 1887, Benz built three versions of the car. Bertha Benz made her road trip in Model III.

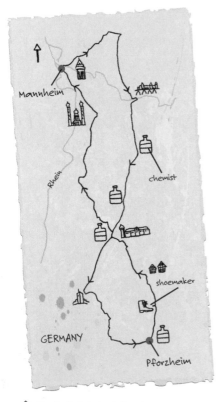

↑ Bertha's trip took her from Mannheim to Pforzheim and back. In 2008, the Bertha Benz Memorial Route opened so that people could retrace her journey.

→ The Benz Patent Motorwagen was uncomfortable for Bertha to drive compared to cars today. The wheels had solid rubber tires, which made the ride bumpy.

↑ On their journey, Bertha and her sons had to push the car up hills. Karl Benz later added a lower gear to make traveling uphill easier.

Bertha and her sons, Eugen and Richard, pushed the car away from the house to avoid waking Karl. Then they started it up and set off. First they headed in the wrong direction, but they got back on the right track. There were no smooth pavement roads, no signposts, no gas stations and no car mechanics. Bertha had to use her wits to overcome all these obstacles.

The car ran on ligroin, which was a stain remover as well as a fuel. Bertha bought it over the counter in chemists. She also took water from streams and rivers and frequently poured it over the engine to cool it down. When the car broke down, Bertha quickly came up with solutions. She jabbed her hat pin into a fuel pipe to unblock it and wrapped clothing around an ignition wire that had become exposed. During the journey, the brakes wore out so she visited a local shoemaker who covered them in leather, thus inventing brake lining.

When they reached Pforzheim, Bertha sent a telegram to her husband. News of the car journey had already hit the press. Everyone had heard about it – Bertha had achieved her goal. The next year, Karl started manufacturing the first cars for the public. Soon, other people were doing the same and sales took off. By the early 20th century, the motor car was well on its way to becoming one of the most popular types of transport in the world.

EXTRA

THE NEED FOR SPEED

Karl's first car only reached 16 km (10 miles) per hour. But he went on to build much more powerful machines.

In 1911, Karl's **Blitzen Benz**, set a land speed record of 228.1 km (141.7 miles) per hour. The front of the car was shaped like a bird's beak. Its record held for 8 years.

One of Benz's most famous racing cars was the 1923 **Teardrop**. With a revolutionary streamlined body shaped like a teardrop, it could travel at speeds of more than 140 km (90 miles) per hour.

In 1896, Benz designed a **flat engine** for improved stability and control. It is still used today in high-performance Porsche and Subaru cars and in some racecars.

HUMANS TAKE TO THE AIR

THE BIG IDEA	» To build an airplane that could soar safely through the skies, making the dream of human flight a reality.
CHALLENGES Danger of crashes; other inventors trying to get there first; long battles in court	**WHAT** **WRIGHT FLYER** **WHO** Orville and Wilbur Wright **WHERE** Dayton, Ohio and Kitty Hawk, North Carolina, USA **WHEN** 1903 to 1908 **HOW** by testing and improving their designs **WHY** the brothers were fascinated with flying from childhood
BACKGROUND	Unpowered flying machines, such as gliders and hot-air balloons, had already been invented. The Wright Brothers wanted to create a powered aircraft that a pilot could control.

NAME: Orville Wright
BORN: August 19, 1871
DIED: age 76
NATIONALITY: American
JOB: engineer, pilot
FAMOUS FOR: developing the Wright Flyer and making its first ever controlled flight

INVENTION ❶

Built the first practical airplane and designed features that are still used today to keep planes steady in the air.

INVENTION ❷

Made the first successful controlled flights in an airplane powered by an engine.

NAME: Wilbur Wright
BORN: April 16, 1867
DIED: age 45
NATIONALITY: American
JOB: inventor, pilot
FAMOUS FOR: inventing the Wright Flyer and piloting it alongside his brother

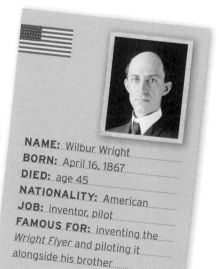

→ An illustration of the Wright Brothers' first successful flight. Orville Wright balances precariously on his stomach to control the plane. There was no cockpit for the pilot.

HUMANS TAKE TO THE AIR

≫ Could the Wright Brothers get their airplane in the air? And keep it there?

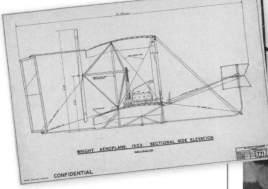

↑ A detailed plan of the first *Wright Flyer*. The brothers analyzed all the data from their experiments to work out the best design for their flying machines. They continually improved their airplanes.

Orville Wright said
'If we worked on the assumption that what is accepted as true really is true, then there would be little hope for advance.'

↑ On December 17, 1903, Orville sent a telegram home to his father to let him know that the flights that day had been successful. The brothers were secretive and wanted to be sure of success before they told the newspapers.

↑ Wilbur Wright takes his sister Katherine for a ride in one of the brothers' planes. She has string tied around her wide skirt to stop it from flapping in the air.

Wilbur and Orville Wright were fascinated by flying machines. As children they built toy helicopters powered by rubber bands and made kites to sell to their friends. In their twenties, they opened a bicycle shop and put any spare money towards their flying experiments. Soon they were flying gliders, improving designs and developing their skills as pilots. By 1903, they had built the *Wright Flyer* – an aircraft powered by an engine. The brothers were ready and eager to test out their brand-new machine.

Late in the year, they traveled to Kitty Hawk, North Carolina to begin their tests. But the propeller on the back of the plane broke and had to be repaired. Then bad weather set in. The Wright Brothers were stuck on the ground in a basic, uncomfortable camp, getting more and more frustrated. Finally, on December 14, 1903, the clouds lifted and there was a chance for their aircraft to take to the skies. Orville and Wilbur tossed a coin to see who would be the pilot. It was a tense moment – the winner could be the first person to fly a powered airplane successfully, but he would also be risking his life for the honor. The older brother, Wilbur, won the toss and climbed aboard the wooden flying machine.

The airplane took off and rose quickly, then slowed and stalled in mid-air. It fell back down, sinking into the sandy ground. The first flight had not been a success. Still, the brothers were hopeful. Their plane had taken off well – they just needed to keep it in the air.

Three days later, on December 17, despite gusting winds, they tried again with Orville at the controls. As the plane lifted, Wilbur encouraged the ground crew to cheer and shout, building up his brother's confidence. The *Wright Flyer* climbed and dived sharply as before, bucking like a wild horse, but this time it stayed in the air. Orville flew for 12 seconds and traveled 37 m (121 ft), then landed safely. Everyone cheered wildly. This short successful flight had changed history and would go on to change the way people traveled all over the world.

↑ Wilbur on board the first *Wright Flyer*. To steer the plane he lay flat in a cradle, which had wires attached to the wings, and swiveled his hips.

That day, the brothers took turns to fly another three times. The fourth flight, piloted by Wilbur, lasted 59 seconds and covered 260 m (853 ft). Wilbur landed perfectly, but then a sudden gust of wind threw the plane across the sand. It rolled over and over until it was nothing but a heap of broken wood and torn cloth. The first *Wright Flyer* was no more, but it had achieved its aim and the brothers were delighted.

HUMANS TAKE TO THE AIR

≫ Could the Wright Brothers get their airplane in the air? And keep it there?

▶▶ HOW TO ...

Make a Paper Dart Plane
You will need: paper

----- crease   ← fold

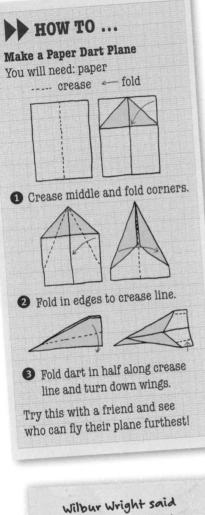

1 Crease middle and fold corners.

2 Fold in edges to crease line.

3 Fold dart in half along crease line and turn down wings.

Try this with a friend and see who can fly their plane furthest!

Wilbur Wright said
'I confess that in 1901 I said to my brother Orville that man would not fly for fifty years ...'

Orville and Wilbur went back home to Dayton, Ohio and set to work building a new and improved version of the plane, the *Wright Flyer II*. It was a close copy of the first model with a more powerful engine and a few altered features. In September 1904, after several rocky attempts, the brothers mastered how to turn the plane in the air and Orville flew in a complete circle for the first time.

The *Wright Flyer II* still had control problems though, so the brothers took the plane apart and built yet another model, the *Wright Flyer III*. This plane was a huge leap forward. On October 5, 1905, Wilbur flew for 39 km (24 miles) and stayed in the air for 38 minutes. He was only forced to land because the engine ran out of fuel. The flight was longer than all of the brothers' flights in 1903 and 1904 put together.

↑ A postcard from around 1905 showing the *Wright Flyer III* in action.

STORY OF AIR TRAVEL	1903	1909	1927	1932
There have been many developments in air travel since the Wright Brothers' historic first flight. Today, passenger planes criss-cross the skies all day and night, faster and safer than ever before.	The Wright Brothers achieve the world's first powered flight in a heavier-than-air vehicle.	Louis Blériot crosses the English Channel in an aircraft.	Charles Lindbergh makes a solo non-stop flight across the Atlantic Ocean.	Amelia Earhart becomes the first woman to fly across the Atlantic Ocean.

↑ During one demonstration of the *Wright Flyer III*, Orville had a bad crash. He was lucky to escape with his life. His passenger, Thomas Selfridge, was killed.

↑ The wingspan of this modern *Boeing 747* jumbo jet is longer than the entire distance covered by the Wright Brothers' first successful powered flight.

By now, Orville and Wilbur were sure they had invented a practical aircraft, but officials doubted their claims because they let so few people watch their flights. Meanwhile, other inventors were building planes, too. So, in 1908, the brothers staged a series of demonstrations in Europe and the USA. The dazzling displays thrilled the crowds and proved that the brothers were miles ahead of the competition. Orville and Wilbur became world-famous. After adding seats for the pilot and a passenger, they began to sell their planes successfully.

↑ *Skylon* is a new kind of aircraft, called a space plane, that is in development. It will take off from a runway and fly at high speed into space to launch satellites or take cargo to the International Space Station.

Wilbur Wright died in 1912 after a short illness, but Orville lived into old age. By the time of Orville's death in 1948, passenger planes were carrying people all over the world and a new aircraft had just traveled faster than the speed of sound.

1933	1937	1947	1976	1986	2014
The *Boeing 247* airliner makes its first flight. It can carry 10 passengers.	Frank Whittle and Hans von Ohain each develop jet engines, making planes fly faster.	Chuck Yeager goes supersonic in the *X-1* plane, travelling faster than the speed of sound.	Supersonic airliner *Concorde* makes its first passenger flight.	Dick Rutan and Jeana Yeager fly around the world without stopping or refueling.	Development work continues on space plane *Skylon*, with test flights planned for 2019.

THE FIRST WORKING
TELESCOPE

THE BIG IDEA	» To build a marvelous new instrument that could make things appear larger than they actually were.
CHALLENGES Unable to get a patent for his device; struggled to make his telescope really powerful	**WHAT** REFRACTING TELESCOPE **WHO** Hans Lippershey **WHERE** Middelburg, Netherlands **WHEN** 1608 **HOW** by enclosing two different-shaped glass lenses in a tube **WHY** so that people could study things far away in more detail
BACKGROUND	Armies were thrilled by Lippershey's invention because it let them keep a lookout for enemies and protect an area from attack. Later, astronomers developed the telescope to study objects in space.

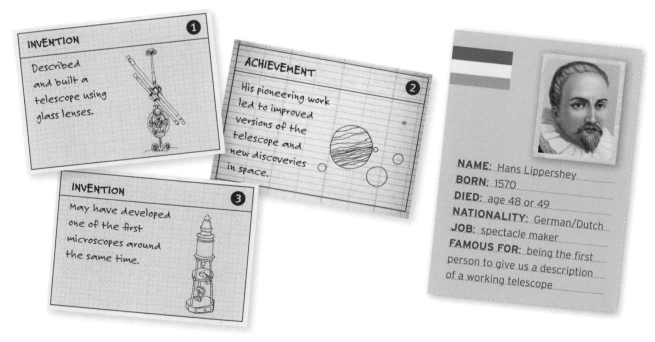

INVENTION ❶
Described and built a telescope using glass lenses.

ACHIEVEMENT ❷
His pioneering work led to improved versions of the telescope and new discoveries in space.

INVENTION ❸
May have developed one of the first microscopes around the same time.

NAME: Hans Lippershey
BORN: 1570
DIED: age 48 or 49
NATIONALITY: German/Dutch
JOB: spectacle maker
FAMOUS FOR: being the first person to give us a description of a working telescope

→ Lippershey's telescope was a small instrument that you could hold up to your eye, but as refracting telescopes became more powerful they also got bigger. This illustration shows the enormous Great Lick Refractor built in the 1880s.

THE FIRST WORKING TELESCOPE

Lenses that curve outward are called convex lenses. They help people to see things better close up. Concave lenses curve inward. They let people see things better far away.

Hans Lippershey was one of several spectacle makers in the Netherlands in the early 1600s. By this time, glasses were fairly common and many people with poor eyesight bought them to make reading easier or to see things far away more clearly. There is little information about Lippershey's life, but we do know that his work grinding lenses for spectacles led him to develop an incredible new instrument. Today, we call it the refracting telescope. Several other people developed telescopes around the same time but Lippershey gave us the first written record of the device.

One story tells us that Lippershey was in his shop when his son started playing with the glass lenses on the counter. The boy picked up a convex lens and a concave lens, and looked through them both at the same time. Suddenly, the church tower in the distance appeared much bigger and clearer than before. He ran to tell his father, who enclosed the lenses at opposite ends of a tube to create the telescope. In October 1608, Lippershey applied for a patent, a document from the government that would protect his device from copycats. Within a few weeks, two other lens makers did the same.

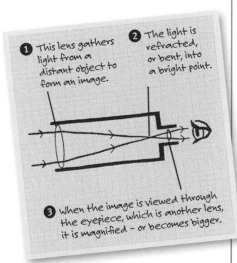

1. This lens gathers light from a distant object to form an image.
2. The light is refracted, or bent, into a bright point.
3. When the image is viewed through the eyepiece, which is another lens, it is magnified – or becomes bigger.

In a refracting telescope, lenses work together to collect light.

Newton's telescope

Galileo's telescope

→ Galileo and Newton used their telescopes to study the skies. Galileo improved Lippershey's design to build the first powerful refracting telescope.

ADVANCES IN TELESCOPES	1608 (October 2)	1608 (late October)	1609	1611
This timeline highlights how telescopes have changed over the ages. Today, scientists no longer use refracting telescopes but they are popular with people who study the stars as a hobby.	Hans Lippershey describes the first working refracting telescope.	Dutch lens makers Jacob Metius and Zacharias Janssen describe similar instruments.	Galileo Galilei uses Lippershey's ideas to build a more powerful refracting telescope.	Johannes Kepler improves Galileo's design by using two convex lenses.

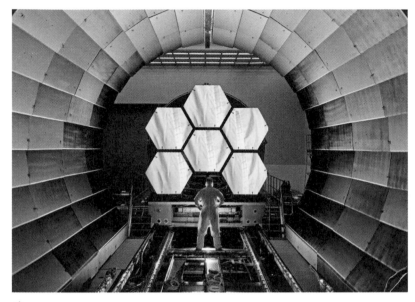

↑ In 2002, technical work began on the James Webb Space Telescope. Here, a scientist checks the huge mirrors that let the telescope see deep into space.

↑ Galileo was the first person to study the Moon's features through a telescope based on Lippershey's design. Today, a small crater on the Moon is named after Lippershey.

The Dutch government did not give Lippershey the patent because it was not clear who had invented the telescope. But an instrument that made things far away appear closer was extremely useful because it let soldiers spy on enemies from a distance. The government asked Lippershey to make 'spyglasses', paid him well, and he lived out his life comfortably.

Perhaps more importantly, though, in Italy the astronomer Galileo read about Lippershey's telescope. Lippershey's instrument could make things appear only three times bigger than their original size, but Galileo built a telescope that could magnify things over 30 times. With it, he studied the Sun, Moon, stars and planets, and he changed the way people thought about the Earth in space forever. It was the first of many incredible discoveries made with a telescope.

↑ Galileo shows his new telescope to officials. He used discoveries made with this telescope to prove that the Sun, rather than the Earth, is at the center of our Solar System, or group of planets.

1655	1668	1897	1990	2007	2018 onward
Christiaan Huygens builds the most powerful refractor of the time and studies Saturn's rings.	Isaac Newton builds a reflecting telescope. It uses mirrors instead of lenses.	Alvan Clark builds the largest and last refractor for scientific study, the Yerkes Telescope.	The Hubble Space Telescope is launched to study deep space. It is a reflecting telescope.	GTC, the world's largest reflecting ground telescope, begins to study the skies.	The James Webb Space Telescope is planned to launch.

LISTENING INTO SPACE

## THE BIG IDEA	⟫ To study the invisible radio waves used for long-distance radio communication.
## CHALLENGES Long hours with painstaking, detailed research; unable to continue his project	**WHAT** **RADIO ANTENNA** **WHO** Karl Jansky **WHERE** Bell Telephone Laboratories, New Jersey, United States **WHEN** 1933 **HOW** he recorded signals, then analyzed the information **WHY** to investigate noises that might interfere with radio messages
## BACKGROUND	During the 1930s wireless radio communication was still in development. While Jansky was trying to improve the system, he made a discovery that would change how we study space.

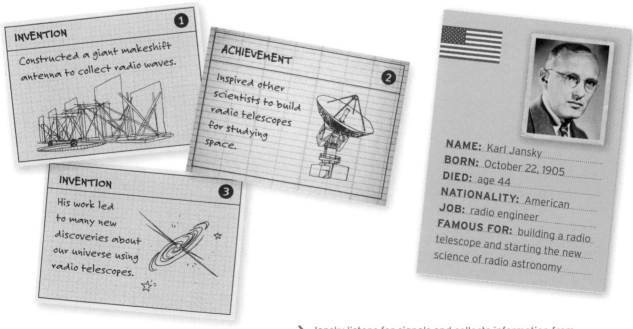

INVENTION ❶
Constructed a giant makeshift antenna to collect radio waves.

ACHIEVEMENT ❷
Inspired other scientists to build radio telescopes for studying space.

INVENTION ❸
His work led to many new discoveries about our universe using radio telescopes.

NAME: Karl Jansky
BORN: October 22, 1905
DIED: age 44
NATIONALITY: American
JOB: radio engineer
FAMOUS FOR: building a radio telescope and starting the new science of radio astronomy

→ Jansky listens for signals and collects information from a printout. Through his investigations, he discovered that our galaxy, the Milky Way, gives off radio waves.

≫ Where was the faint hiss coming from? Jansky wanted to find out ...

↑ The Milky Way is our galaxy, or group of stars. It contains the planets including Earth, the Sun and billions of other stars. From Earth, the Milky Way looks like a faint band of light in the sky.

In May 1933 an article appeared in the *New York Times* newspaper, causing a sensation. It explained that there was a noise coming from outer space that had been traced to the center of our galaxy, the Milky Way. Several days later, people tuned into the radio to listen to the strange hiss being broadcast live. This 'star noise' was discovered by radio engineer Karl Jansky, almost by chance.

Jansky worked for the Bell Telephone Laboratories and was asked to investigate noises that might interfere with radio communications and telephone calls. He built a makeshift antenna out of metal pipes and wood to pick up the sounds, and set it up in the potato fields outside the lab. Then he sat in a shed next door recording and listening. He began to group the noises. Jansky decided that many of the pops and clicks came from local and distant thunderstorms, but there was also a steady weak hiss. After spending more than a year collecting information and making calculations, he pinpointed the hiss to the center of the Milky Way. He had found evidence that our galaxy was giving off radio waves.

↑ Four years after Jansky built his radio antenna, astronomer Grote Reber picked up his research and built a dish-shaped radio telescope in his back garden. Radio astronomy began to take off.

'In my estimation, it was obvious that Jansky had made a fundamental and very important discovery.'
Grote Reber

↑ Jansky's radio antenna had wheels underneath so that it could spin around on a track. The other engineers nicknamed it Jansky's Merry-Go-Round.

↑ Radio telescopes usually work together to collect signals. This group in New Mexico is named the Karl G Jansky Very Large Array in honour of the scientist.

Jansky wanted to continue his research and suggested building a more sensitive dish antenna, similar to a modern-day radio telescope. But his discovery had no use for radio or telephone communication, so the project ended. He went on to different research, then died from an illness in 1950 at age 44. It was left to other pioneering scientists to develop his work.

By the late 1950s, radio telescopes were listening into space and radio astronomy had become a whole new science. A radio telescope can detect objects in the universe hidden from our eyes. The instrument has led to some amazing discoveries, including new space objects such as pulsars and quasars. With radio telescopes we are mapping the structure of the Milky Way, discovering how stars are born and die, starting to understand black holes and learning more about how the universe began. Although Jansky never lived to see it, he opened the door to a new way for us to study space.

← This is the Crab Nebula, a cloud of dust and gas in the Milky Way. At its center, there is a pulsar, or pulsating star. Jocelyn Bell Burnell discovered the first pulsar in 1967, using a radio telescope.

BUILDING SPACE
ROCKETS

THE BIG IDEA	≫ To design the world's biggest rocket, powerful enough to launch astronauts to the Moon.

CHALLENGES	**WHAT** ***SATURN V* ROCKET**
	WHO Wernher von Braun
	WHERE Marshall Space Flight Center, Alabama, United States
Needed over 3 million parts; hugely expensive; a race against another nation	**WHEN** 1958 to 1969
	HOW von Braun led a world-class team of engineers and scientists
	WHY to be first to the Moon and make a childhood dream come true

BACKGROUND	In the 1950s, there was a race between the Soviet Union and the United States to reach space. In 1961, the Soviets sent the first man into space. The United States fought back by sending astronauts to the Moon.

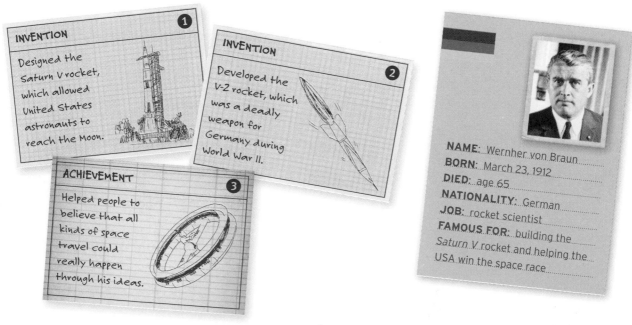

INVENTION ❶
Designed the Saturn V rocket, which allowed United States astronauts to reach the Moon.

INVENTION ❷
Developed the V-2 rocket, which was a deadly weapon for Germany during World War II.

ACHIEVEMENT ❸
Helped people to believe that all kinds of space travel could really happen through his ideas.

NAME: Wernher von Braun
BORN: March 23, 1912
DIED: age 65
NATIONALITY: German
JOB: rocket scientist
FAMOUS FOR: building the Saturn V rocket and helping the USA win the space race

→ The *Saturn V* rocket was von Braun's greatest achievement. Today, it is still one of the most complex and powerful rockets ever made. It was higher than a 36-story building.

BUILDING SPACE
ROCKETS

≫ The *Saturn V* rocket was a technical masterpiece. But was it safe?

↑ Von Braun developed the impressive but lethal *V-2* rocket for the German army when he was still in his 20s. During World War II, more than 3,000 *V-2* rockets were launched against enemies.

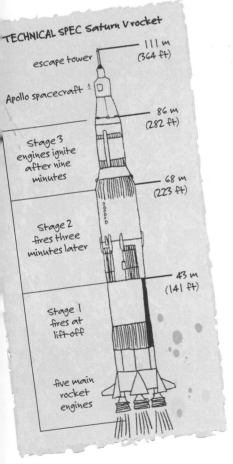

TECHNICAL SPEC Saturn V rocket

- escape tower — 111 m (364 ft)
- Apollo spacecraft
- — 86 m (282 ft)
- Stage 3 engines ignite after nine minutes
- — 68 m (223 ft)
- Stage 2 fires three minutes later
- — 43 m (141 ft)
- Stage 1 fires at lift-off
- five main rocket engines

↑ The *Saturn V* rocket was divided into three sections called stages. Each stage had its own engines and fuel. When the fuel was used up, the stages fell away.

↑ Von Braun leans over to talk to his colleagues at the Marshall Space Flight Center. He and his team carried out most of the Apollo Moon mission research here.

On July 16, 1969, three American astronauts sat in a cramped Apollo spacecraft perched upon a giant *Saturn V* rocket. They were about to blast off to the Moon. If they made it, they would be the first people ever to walk across its dusty surface. The whole world watched and held its breath. This towering steel tube was loaded with 3.5 million liters (924,600 gallons) of deadly liquid fuel – enough to fill almost one and a half Olympic-sized swimming pools. Would it lift off or explode in a burning fireball?

It had taken von Braun and his top-notch team over ten years to get to this point. During World War II, he was a rocket designer in Germany. Afterwards, he worked for the United States, first building military missiles and then switching to spaceflight. His team developed several *Saturn* rockets with a Moon mission in mind. The earlier rockets were smaller and used for tests and planning. By the time *Saturn V* was ready, it weighed 2.8 million kilograms (6.2 million pounds) – it was as heavy as a herd of 400 elephants!

The Apollo Moon mission was a huge success. On July 20, 1969, Neil Armstrong and 'Buzz' Aldrin touched down on the lunar surface while Michael Collins watched from above. From 1969 to 1972, *Saturn V* blasted off six more times, landing a total of 12 people on the Moon. In 1973, on its final outing, it launched the *Skylab* space station into orbit.

↑ Astronaut 'Buzz' Aldrin stands on the Moon next to the United States flag.

From an early age, Wernher von Braun had a passion to build rockets. But the first rockets he developed were used as weapons. Although they were incredible feats of engineering, they killed many people. Later in life he turned his attention to space exploration, another childhood passion. This led him to become the inventor of probably the most inspirational rocket of all time. Braun also dreamt of building a wheel-shaped space station above the Earth. That hasn't happened, but we do have astronauts living and working on the International Space Station today.

The International Space Station circles the Earth day and night. →

INSPIRING INVENTIONS

Humans constantly invent and develop things. Sometimes inventions change the world! It's impossible to include everything invented in one book, but here are a few more examples to inspire you.

INVENTIONS BY MISTAKE

Not all inventions come about through detailed research. Sometimes a mistake or an accident can surprise us.

WHAT PENICILLIN
WHO Alexander Fleming
In 1928, Fleming left a sample dish on his workbench instead of putting it away. He noticed that a penicillin mold had grown there, with a germ-free area around it. He had discovered the first antibiotic, or bacteria-killer.

WHAT CORN FLAKES
WHO John Harvey Kellogg and Will Keith Kellogg
In 1894, the Kellogg brothers were interrupted while baking wheat and it went stale. They tried to roll it into a dough but ended up with flakes, which they toasted. It tasted so good that they did the same with corn.

WHAT MICROWAVE OVEN
WHO Percy Spencer
The microwave oven was invented in the 1940s. Spencer was researching radar and experimenting with high-power microwave beams. A chocolate bar melted in his pocket and he realized that the beams could be used to heat food.

WHAT VELCRO
WHO George Mestral
In 1948, Mestral thought of the fabric fastener, Velcro, after his dog got seed burrs stuck in its fur. He examined them under a microscope and applied the idea to fabric.

TEENAGE INVENTIONS

Experienced scientists and engineers aren't the only people who invent things. Young people can be great inventors, too!

WHAT TRAMPOLINE
WHO George Nissen
In 1930, Nissen was 16 years old and a keen gymnast. He visited the circus and watched trapeze artists bounce onto the safety net at the end of their act. It inspired him to start developing the trampoline in his parents' garage.

WHAT BLISSYMBOL PRINTER
WHO Rachel Zimmerman
In the 1980s, schoolgirl Zimmerman developed software to help people with physical disabilities and who could not speak to send emails. They pointed to symbols and her 'printer' translated them into written sentences.

WHAT WINDSURFING BOARD
WHO Peter Chilvers
As a young boy, Chilvers enjoyed water sports. One day in 1958, on the south coast of England, he attached a sail to his surfboard and became the first known windsurfer. He was 12 years old at the time.

WHAT BRAILLE
WHO Louis Braille
By the time he was 15 years old, Louis Braille had developed a way for blind people to read using raised dots on a page. Braille had been blind himself since the age of three. His system, created around 1824, is still used today worldwide.

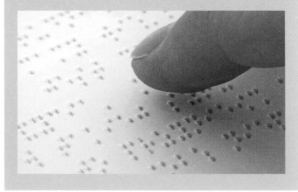

INVENTIONS BY WOMEN

In the past there were fewer opportunities for women to become scientists or inventors. Things have changed in more recent times.

WHAT LASERPHACO PROBE
WHO Patricia E Bath
Bath is a pioneering African-American inventor. In 1981 she developed the laserphaco probe, which is used to treat cataracts, a condition that causes blindness. Her surgical instrument has restored sight to many people.

WHAT CIRCULAR SAW
WHO Tabitha Babbitt
Babbitt was part of a religious community called the Shakers, who lived simply and made their own furniture. In 1813 she devised a saw with a spinning toothed blade, which made cutting wood easier. It is a popular tool today.

WHAT COBOL PROGRAMMING LANGUAGE
WHO Grace Murray Hopper
Hopper played a large part in developing the COBOL programming language between 1959 and 1961. It's still used for many business computers. She also coined the phrase 'debugging', which means fixing computer problems.

WHAT WINDSCREEN WIPER
WHO Mary Anderson
In 1903, Anderson registered a device for the automatic cleaning of car windows. She was inspired to make windscreen wipers after seeing a tram traveling with the front window open to stop sleet from settling.

WHAT GEOBOND
WHO Patricia Billings
Geobond is a virtually indestructible, fireproof material used for buildings, aircrafts and bridges. Billings, a sculptor, started developing it in the 1970s when she dropped one of her works of art and it shattered.

UNUSUAL INVENTIONS

Some inventions seem bizarre and don't always take off. But they may lead us to new and better ideas.

WHAT RADIO HAT
WHO Victor Hoeflich
Before portable radios, headphones and MP3 players, there was the radio hat. Launched in 1949, it was a helmet with a built-in radio so you could listen to music on the move. It had a short run of success.

WHAT WATER BICYCLE
WHO Mohammed Saidullah
In 1975, when his village flooded, Indian inventor Saidullah attached floats and propeller-like blades to a bicycle so he could travel across water as well as land. It was an ingenious solution to an immediate problem.

WHAT MONOCYCLE
WHO M. Goventosa
Since the 1860s, people have experimented with one-wheeled motorcycles. This version was made by Italian inventor Goventosa in the 1930s. They have never really caught on other than for fun.

WHAT ITER-AUTO ROUTE FINDER
WHO Unknown
The Italian Iter-Auto was an ingenious idea from the days before GPS in cars. Designed in the 1930s, the device was attached to your speedometer and contained a paper map that scrolled down as you traveled.

WHAT *SINCLAIR C5*
WHO Clive Sinclair
Launched in 1985, the *Sinclair C5* was an electric vehicle for one person. It was a huge failure. Today, it is a collector's item. Electric cars do not pollute the air and are now more popular. They could become the cars of the future.

GLOSSARY

Allied Forces
One of the two opposing sides in World War II, made up of many countries including the United Kingdom, the United States and the Soviet Union.

alternating current
The type of electricity usually used to supply power to homes and businesses.

antenna
A wire rod used to transmit or receive radio or television signals.

antibiotic
A drug, such as penicillin, used to kill bacteria and heal infections.

Armed Forces
The army, navy and air force of a particular country.

Artificial Intelligence
A branch of science that tries to make computers behave like humans.

astronomer
A person who studies space.

carbon
A chemical element found in all living things, including materials such as coal and wood.

celluloid
A type of plastic that was used in the past to film movies.

chemical
A substance – solid, liquid, gas or a mixture – that is either man-made or occurs naturally.

chemist
A person who carries out research and experiments using chemicals.

cog
A toothed wheel that fits with another matching wheel to transfer movement. Cogs are also called cogwheels or gears.

condenser
A device that changes a gas or vapor to a liquid, such as steam to water, usually by cooling.

cosmonaut
A Russian astronaut.

crank
A bar with a handle that can be turned to move something.

crankshaft
A rod that turns up-and-down movement into circular movement, for example to make a wheel turn.

crater
A large bowl-shaped dip in the ground. There are many craters on the Moon.

cylinder
A tube-shaped object that is often the working part of an engine.

documentary
A programme that gives information about real people and events.

electricity
The energy that travels along wires to make lights, TVs and other things work in the home. Lightning is also a kind of electricity.

engineer
A person trained to design, build and maintain machinery or systems.

filament
A fine thread or wire in a light bulb that heats and glows as electricity passes through it.

fluorescent light
A bright lamp made of a long glass tube with a glowing gas inside.

furnace
A large, hot enclosed fire used for making steam, melting metals or heating a building.

galaxy
An enormous group of stars, dust and gas in space. Our galaxy, the Milky Way, includes our solar system and billions of other stars.

generator
A machine that produces electricity from other forms of power.

glider
An aircraft designed to fly without an engine.

humanoid
Having the appearance and character of a human.

ignite
To set something alight.

ignition
The system for making electric sparks to start the fuel burning in a car engine.

Industrial Revolution
A rapid period of change in the 18th and 19th centuries when factories appeared and people started to make many more goods by machine.

irrigate
To supply an area with water, often for crops, using channels and pipes.

jet engine
A type of powerful engine, used in airplanes, that sends out a jet of heated air and gases to move the airplane forward.

lens
A curved piece of glass or plastic that makes objects look bigger when you look through it.

lever
A bar resting on a pivot, which provides extra force to lift or move a heavy object.

locomotive
An engine for pulling trains. The first locomotives were powered by steam.

methodical
Orderly.

missile
A weapon that can be fired over long distances and explodes on landing.

nebula
A cloudy patch far away in space, made up of dust and gas.

particle
A tiny object. Molecules, atoms and electrons are all particles.

patent
A document from the government that gives only the inventor the right to make and sell their product for a set period of time.

piston
A disc that slides up and down inside a tube that is used to make parts of an engine move.

pulley
A wheel with a rope around it, used for lifting heavy loads.

pulsar
A type of star in space that gives off pulses of radio waves.

radio astronomy
The science of studying objects in space, which give off radio waves.

radio waves
Electrical waves that travel through the air. They can be made naturally by lightning and objects in space or produced artificially by humans.

receiver
A device, such as a TV set, that receives radio or TV signals.

refract
To make a ray of light change direction.

revolutionary
Causing a complete change.

satellite
An object sent into space that circles the Earth and sends back information.

solar system
The Sun and all the objects that go around it, including the Earth and the rest of the planets.

Soviet Union
The former name given to a group of countries including Russia and 14 others.

space probe
An unmanned spacecraft that carries instruments to investigate planets, moons and deep space.

suction pump
A pump that can draw liquid through a pipe into a chamber.

supersonic
Faster than the speed of sound.

telegraph
A system for sending messages along electrical wires or with radio signals.

transmitter
A device that sends out radio or TV signals.

visionary
Having original and inventive ideas about what the future could be like.

voltage
The force of an electric current, measured in volts.

volume
The amount of space an object or substance takes up.

web browser
A computer software program that lets you search and find information on the World Wide Web.

INDEX

On the cover:
Front above and spine: Drawing of the Incandescent Light Bulb (detail) by Thomas Edison, 1880.
Photo: United States National Archives and Records Administration, College Park, Maryland.
Front above left: Wright Brothers' airplane c. 1905. Photo: NMPFT/Daily Herald Archive/Science and Society Picture Library.
Front above right: Experiments with Mirrors and the Sun's Rays (details from book illustration). Photo: Science Museum/Science and Society Picture Library.
Back: Postcard advertising the Cinoscope, 1920–29. Photo: Collection IM/Kharbine-Tapabor/The Art Archive.

Genius! © 2015 Thames & Hudson Ltd, London

Designed by Karen Wilks

Consultant: Jane Insley

First published in 2015 in hardcover in the United States of America by Thames & Hudson Inc.,
500 Fifth Avenue, New York, New York 10110

thamesandhudsonusa.com

Library of Congress Catalog Card Number 2014952828
ISBN 978-0-500-65043-1

Printed and bound in China by Everbest Printing Co. Ltd